Date Due

JAN 29			
DEC 17			

PERSONALITY DISORDERS

GENERAL EDITORS

Dale C. Garell, M.D.
Medical Director, California Children Services, Department of Health
  Services, County of Los Angeles
Associate Dean for Curriculum
Clinical Professor, Department of Pediatrics & Family Medicine,
  University of Southern California School of Medicine
Former President, Society for Adolescent Medicine

Solomon H. Snyder, M.D.
Distinguished Service Professor of Neuroscience, Pharmacology, and
  Psychiatry, Johns Hopkins University School of Medicine
Former president, Society of Neuroscience
Albert Lasker Award in Medical Research, 1978

CONSULTING EDITORS

Robert W. Blum, M.D., Ph.D.
Associate Professor, School of Public Health and Department of
  Pediatrics
Director, Adolescent Health Program, University of Minnesota
Consultant, World Health Organization

Charles E. Irwin, Jr., M.D.
Associate Professor of Pediatrics; Director, Division of Adolescent
  Medicine, University of California, San Francisco

Lloyd J. Kolbe, Ph.D.
Chief, Office of School Health & Special Projects, Center for Health
  Promotion & Education, Centers for Disease Control
President, American School Health Association

Jordan J. Popkin
Director, Division of Federal Employee Occupational Health, U.S. Public
  Health Service Region I

Joseph L. Rauh, M.D.
Professor of Pediatrics and Medicine, Adolescent Medicine, Children's
  Hospital Medical Center, Cincinnati
Former president, Society for Adolescent Medicine

THE ENCYCLOPEDIA OF
H E A L T H

PSYCHOLOGICAL DISORDERS
AND THEIR TREATMENT

Solomon H. Snyder, M.D. · General Editor

PERSONALITY DISORDERS

Bruce Friedland

Introduction by C. Everett Koop, M.D., Sc.D.
former Surgeon General, U.S. Public Health Service

CHELSEA HOUSE PUBLISHERS
New York · Philadelphia

ON THE COVER Frau, Kopf Stützend, 1907, Emil Nolde, lithograph with watercolor
wash.

Chelsea House Publishers
EDITOR-IN-CHIEF Remmel Nunn
MANAGING EDITOR Karyn Gullen Browne
COPY CHIEF Juliann Barbato
PICTURE EDITOR Adrian G. Allen
ART DIRECTOR Maria Epes
DEPUTY COPY CHIEF Mark Rifkin
ASSISTANT ART DIRECTOR Loraine Machlin
MANUFACTURING MANAGER Gerald Levine
SYSTEMS MANAGER Rachel Vigier
PRODUCTION MANAGER Joseph Romano
PRODUCTION COORDINATOR Marie Claire Cebrián

The Encyclopedia of Health
SENIOR EDITOR Jake Goldberg

Staff for PERSONALITY DISORDERS
ASSISTANT EDITOR Nicole Bowen
COPY EDITOR Brian Sookram
EDITORIAL ASSISTANT Leigh Hope Wood
PICTURE RESEARCHER Georganne M. Backman
SENIOR DESIGNER Marjorie Zaum
DESIGN ASSISTANT Debora Smith

3 5 7 9 8 6 4

Library of Congress Cataloging-in-Publication Data

Friedland, Bruce.
    Personality disorders/by Bruce Friedland.
      p. cm.—(The Encyclopedia of health)
    Includes bibliographical references.
    Summary: Discusses the diagnosis, effects, and treatment of various personality
disorders, including antisocial, histrionic, dependent, and aggressive personality disorders.
    ISBN 0-7910-0051-6
        0-7910-0531-3 (pbk.)
    1. Personality disorders—Juvenile literature. [1. Personality disorders.]
I. Title. II. Series.   90-1716
RC554.F75 1990   CIP
616.85′8—dc20   AC

CONTENTS

The goal of the ENCYCLOPEDIA OF HEALTH *is to provide general information in
the ever-changing areas of physiology, psychology, and related medical issues.
The titles in this series are not intended to take the place of the professional
advice of a physician or other health care professional.*

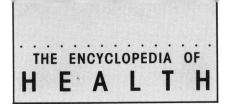

THE ENCYCLOPEDIA OF
H E A L T H

THE HEALTHY BODY

The Circulatory System
Dental Health
The Digestive System
The Endocrine System
Exercise
Genetics & Heredity
The Human Body: An Overview
Hygiene
The Immune System
Memory & Learning
The Musculoskeletal System
The Nervous System
Nutrition
The Reproductive System
The Respiratory System
The Senses
Speech & Hearing
Sports Medicine
Vision
Vitamins & Minerals

THE LIFE CYCLE

Adolescence
Adulthood
Aging
Childhood
Death & Dying
The Family
Friendship & Love
Pregnancy & Birth

MEDICAL ISSUES

Careers in Health Care
Environmental Health
Folk Medicine
Health Care Delivery
Holistic Medicine
Medical Ethics
Medical Fakes & Frauds
Medical Technology
Medicine & the Law
Occupational Health
Public Health

PYSCHOLOGICAL DISORDERS AND THEIR TREATMENT

Anxiety & Phobias
Child Abuse
Compulsive Behavior
Delinquency & Criminal Behavior
Depression
Diagnosing & Treating Mental Illness
Eating Habits & Disorders
Learning Disabilities
Mental Retardation
Personality Disorders
Schizophrenia
Stress Management
Suicide

MEDICAL DISORDERS AND THEIR TREATMENT

AIDS
Allergies
Alzheimer's Disease
Arthritis
Birth Defects
Cancer
The Common Cold
Diabetes
Emergency Medicine
Gynecological Disorders
Headaches
The Hospital
Kidney Disorders
Medical Diagnosis
The Mind-Body Connection
Mononucleosis and Other Infectious Diseases
Nuclear Medicine
Organ Transplants
Pain
Physical Handicaps
Poisons & Toxins
Prescription & OTC Drugs
Sexually Transmitted Diseases
Skin Disorders
Stroke & Heart Disease
Substance Abuse
Tropical Medicine

PREVENTION AND EDUCATION: THE KEYS TO GOOD HEALTH

C. Everett Koop, M.D., Sc.D.
former Surgeon General,
U.S. Public Health Service

The issue of health education has received particular attention in recent years because of the presence of AIDS in the news. But our response to this particular tragedy points up a number of broader issues that doctors, public health officials, educators, and the public face. In particular, it points up the necessity for sound health education for citizens of all ages.

Over the past 25 years this country has been able to bring about dramatic declines in the death rates for heart disease, stroke, accidents, and, for people under the age of 45, cancer. Today, Americans generally eat better and take better care of themselves than ever before. Thus, with the help of modern science and technology, they have a better chance of surviving serious—even catastrophic—illnesses. That's the good news.

But, like every phonograph record, there's a flip side, and one with special significance for young adults. According to a report issued in 1979 by Dr. Julius Richmond, my predecessor as Surgeon General, Americans aged 15 to 24 had a higher death rate in 1979 than they did 20 years earlier. The causes: violent death and injury, alcohol and drug abuse, unwanted pregnancies, and sexually transmitted diseases. Adolescents are particularly vulnerable because they are beginning to explore their own sexuality and perhaps to experiment with drugs. The need for educating young people is critical, and the price of neglect is high.

Yet even for the population as a whole, our health is still far from what it could be. Why? A 1974 Canadian government report attributed all death and disease to four broad elements: inadequacies in the health care system, behavioral factors or unhealthy life-styles, environmental hazards, and human biological factors.

To be sure, there are diseases that are still beyond the control of even our advanced medical knowledge and techniques. And despite yearnings that are as old as the human race itself, there is no "fountain of youth" to ward off aging and death. Still, there is a solution to many of the problems that undermine sound health. In a word, that solution is prevention. Prevention, which includes health promotion and education, saves lives, improves the quality of life, and, in the long run, saves money.

In the United States, organized public health activities and preventive medicine have a long history. Important milestones include the improvement of sanitary procedures and the development of pasteurized milk in the late 19th century, and the introduction in the mid-20th century of effective vaccines against polio, measles, German measles, mumps, and other once-rampant diseases. Internationally, organized public health efforts began on a wide-scale basis with the International Sanitary Conference of 1851, to which 12 nations sent representatives. The World Health Organization, founded in 1948, continues these efforts under the aegis of the United Nations, with particular emphasis on combatting communicable diseases and the training of health care workers.

Despite these accomplishments, much remains to be done in the field of prevention. For too long, we have had a medical care system that is science- and technology-based, focused, essentially, on illness and mortality. It is now patently obvious that both the social and the economic costs of such a system are becoming insupportable.

Implementing prevention—and its corollaries, health education and promotion—is the job of several groups of people.

First, the medical and scientific professions need to continue basic scientific research, and here we are making considerable progress. But increased concern with prevention will also have a decided impact on how primary care doctors practice medicine. With a shift to health-based rather than morbidity-based medicine, the role of the "new physician" will include a healthy dose of patient education.

Second, practitioners of the social and behavioral sciences—psychologists, economists, city planners—along with lawyers, business leaders, and government officials—must solve the practical and ethical dilemmas confronting us: poverty, crime, civil rights, literacy, education, employment, housing, sanitation, environmental protection, health care delivery systems, and so forth. All of these issues affect public health.

Third is the public at large. We'll consider that very important group in a moment.

Fourth, and the linchpin in this effort, is the public health profession—doctors, epidemiologists, teachers—who must harness the professional expertise of the first two groups and the common sense and cooperation of the third, the public. They must define the problems statistically and qualitatively and then help us set priorities for finding the solutions.

To a very large extent, improving those statistics is the responsibility of every individual. So let's consider more specifically what the role of the individual should be and why health education is so important to that role. First, and most obviously, individuals can protect themselves from illness and injury and thus minimize their need for professional medical care. They can eat nutritious food, get adequate exercise, avoid tobacco, alcohol, and drugs, and take prudent steps to avoid accidents. The proverbial "apple a day keeps the doctor away" is not so far from the truth, after all.

Second, individuals should actively participate in their own medical care. They should schedule regular medical and dental checkups. Should they develop an illness or injury, they should know when to treat themselves and when to seek professional help. To gain the maximum benefit from any medical treatment that they do require, individuals must become partners in that treatment. For instance, they should understand the effects and side effects of medications. I counsel young physicians that there is no such thing as too much information when talking with patients. But the corollary is the patient must know enough about the nuts and bolts of the healing process to understand what the doctor is telling him. That is at least partially the patient's responsibility.

Education is equally necessary for us to understand the ethical and public policy issues in health care today. Sometimes individuals will encounter these issues in making decisions about their own treatment or that of family members. Other citizens may encounter them as jurors in medical malpractice cases. But we all become involved, indirectly, when we elect our public officials, from school board members to the president. Should surrogate parenting be legal? To what extent is drug testing desirable, legal, or necessary? Should there be public funding for family planning, hospitals, various types of medical research, and medical care for the indigent? How should we allocate scant technological resources, such as kidney dialysis and organ transplants? What is the proper role of government in protecting the rights of patients?

What are the broad goals of public health in the United States today? In 1980, the Public Health Service issued a report aptly entitled *Promoting Health—Preventing Disease: Objectives for the Nation.* This report expressed its goals in terms of mortality and in terms of intermediate goals in education and health improvement. It identified 15 major concerns: controlling high blood pressure; improving family planning; improving pregnancy care and infant health; increasing the rate of immunization; controlling sexually transmitted diseases; controlling the presence of toxic agents and radiation in the environment; improving occupational safety and health; preventing accidents; promoting water fluoridation and dental health; controlling infectious diseases; decreasing smoking; decreasing alcohol and drug abuse; improving nutrition; promoting physical fitness and exercise; and controlling stress and violent behavior.

For healthy adolescents and young adults (ages 15 to 24), the specific goal was a 20% reduction in deaths, with a special focus on motor vehicle injuries and alcohol and drug abuse. For adults (ages 25 to 64), the aim was 25% fewer deaths, with a concentration on heart attacks, strokes, and cancers.

Smoking is perhaps the best example of how individual behavior can have a direct impact on health. Today cigarette smoking is recognized as the most important single preventable cause of death in our society. It is responsible for more cancers and more cancer deaths than any other known agent; is a prime risk factor for heart and blood vessel disease, chronic bronchitis, and emphysema; and is a frequent cause of complications in pregnancies and of babies born prematurely, underweight, or with potentially fatal respiratory and cardiovascular problems.

Since the release of the Surgeon General's first report on smoking in 1964, the proportion of adult smokers has declined substantially, from 43% in 1965 to 30.5% in 1985. Since 1965, 37 million people have quit smoking. Although there is still much work to be done if we are to become a "smoke-free society," it is heartening to note that public health and public education efforts—such as warnings on cigarette packages and bans on broadcast advertising—have already had significant effects.

In 1835, Alexis de Tocqueville, a French visitor to America, wrote, "In America the passion for physical well-being is general." Today, as then, health and fitness are front-page items. But with the greater scientific and technological resources now available to us, we are in a far stronger position to make good health care available to everyone. And with the greater technological threats to us as we approach the 21st century, the need to do so is more urgent than ever before. Comprehensive information about basic biology, preventive medicine, medical and surgical treatments, and related ethical and public policy issues can help you arm yourself with the knowledge you need to be healthy throughout your life.

FOREWORD

Solomon H. Snyder, M.D.

Mental disorders represent the number one health problem for the United States and probably for the entire human population. Some studies estimate that approximately one-third of all Americans suffer from some sort of emotional disturbance. Depression of varying severity will affect as many as 20 percent of all of us at one time or another in our lives. Severe anxiety is even more common.

Adolescence is a time of particular susceptibility to emotional problems. Teenagers are undergoing significant changes in their brain as well as their physical structure. The hormones that alter the organs of reproduction during puberty also influence the way we think and feel. At a purely psychological level, adolescents must cope with major upheavals in their lives. After years of not noticing the opposite sex, they find themselves romantically attracted but must painfully learn the skills of social interchange both for superficial, flirtatious relationships and for genuine intimacy. Teenagers must develop new ways of relating to their parents. Adolescents strive for independence. Yet, our society is structured in such a way that teenagers must remain dependent on their parents for many more years. During adolescence, young men and women examine their own intellectual bents and begin to plan the type of higher education and vocation they believe they will find most fulfilling.

Because of all these challenges, teenagers are more emotionally volatile than adults. Passages from extreme exuberance to dejection are common. The emotional distress of completely normal adolescence can be so severe that the same disability in an adult would be labeled as major mental illness. Although most teenagers somehow muddle through and emerge unscathed, a number of problems are more frequent among adolescents than among adults. Many psychological aberrations reflect severe disturbances, although these are sometimes not regarded as "psychiatric." Eating disorders, to which young adults are especially vulnerable, are an example. An extremely large number of teenagers diet to great excess even though they are not overweight. Many of them suffer from a specific disturbance referred to as anorexia nervosa, a form of self-starvation that is just as real a disorder as diabetes. The same is true for those who eat compulsively and then sometimes force themselves to vomit. They may be afflicted with bulimia.

Depression is also surprisingly frequent among adolescents, although its symptoms may be less obvious in young people than they are in adults. And, because suicide occurs most frequently in those suffering from depression, we must be on the lookout for subtle hints of despondency in those close to us. This is especially urgent because teenage suicide is a rapidly worsening national problem.

The volumes on Psychological Disorders and Their Treatment in the ENCYCLOPEDIA OF HEALTH cover the major areas of mental illness, from mild to severe. They also emphasize the means available for getting help. *Anxiety and Phobias, Depression*, and *Schizophrenia* deal specifically with these forms of mental disturbance. *Child Abuse* and *Delinquency and Criminal Behavior* explore abnormalities of behavior that may stem from environmental and social influences as much as from biological or psychological illness. *Personality Disorders* and *Compulsive Behavior* explain how people develop disturbances of their overall personality. *Learning Disabilities* investigates disturbances of the mind that may reflect neurological derangements as much as psychological abnormalities. *Mental Retardation* explains the various causes of this many-sided handicap, including the genetic component, complications during pregnancy, and traumas during birth. *Suicide* discusses the epidemiology of this tragic phenomenon and outlines the assistance available to those who are at risk. *Stress Management* locates the sources of stress in contemporary society and considers formal strategies for coping with it. Finally, *Diagnosing and Treating Mental Illness* explains to the reader how professionals sift through various signs and symptoms to define the exact nature of the various mental disorders and fully describes the most effective means of alleviating them.

Fortunately, when it comes to psychological disorders, knowing the facts is a giant step toward solving the problems.

CHAPTER 1

PERSONALITY: LASTING PATTERNS OF BEHAVIOR

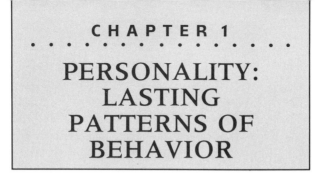

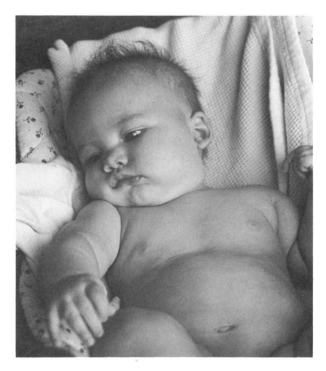

From the moment a person is born, his or her personality begins to take shape. In infancy, childhood, and later in adolescence, the individual explores a multitude of behaviors. Many are rejected, but others, those that prove successful and satisfying, are repeated and eventually become part of a strong and predictable pattern that determines how that person perceives him- or herself and reacts to the surrounding world.

These specific patterns of behavior are key factors in the development of personality. But such deeply ingrained traits can also underlie *personality disorders*, a term psychiatrists and other mental health professionals use to describe behavior patterns that are inflexible and *maladaptive*, that is, marked by poor adjustment to accepted norms. These patterns of behavior can result in emotional upheavals ranging from depression and anxiety to those that spark suicide, and they can cause distress, unhappiness, or even functional impairment for the person with the disorder.

Disorders of personality are so pervasive that their impact on society is often overlooked. Some of history's greatest and most notorious characters were driven by disordered personalities. C. S. Bluemel, author of *War, Politics and Insanity*, writes that "the events of history and the affairs of politics often turn on personality disorders." But people's everyday lives also are often marred by personality disorders—either by having to deal with others with disorders or by having to deal with problems their own disorders have created.

Although symptoms vary for specific personality disorders, the main feature of any disordered personality is an ingrained pattern of inflexible and usually self-defeating behavior. People with personality disorders are locked into certain unsuccessful ways of acting.

Traits such as *paranoia* (experiencing delusions of persecution and feelings of suspiciousness, mistrust, and combativeness); *obsessiveness* (having recurrent, persistent, unwanted thoughts or compulsions); *compulsiveness* (being a perfectionist, rigid, stubborn, and indecisive); *dependency* (reliance on another); and *narcissism* (having exaggerated feelings of self-importance) can be established very early in life. In effect, these maladaptive patterns are programmed into personality and may persist, sometimes with disastrous results, throughout adult life. Most healthy personalities are built on positive, solid foundations. Disordered personalities are built on shaky, negative foundations or on no foundations at all.

Not surprisingly, people with personality disorders have difficulty living a happy, successful life. They often find it difficult to sustain friendships or romantic relationships. They frequently have trouble holding a job or functioning successfully in a social setting, and they can suffer periods of depression or anxiety that

People with personality disorders have deeply ingrained patterns of behavior that make successful social interaction very difficult. Even if these people realize that their behavior causes problems, they are unable to modify it.

may eventually force them to seek professional help. Those with severe symptoms often require hospitalization or end up in prison.

Remarkably, though, the majority of people with personality disorders never seek help because their inflexible and maladaptive traits are so ingrained that they fail to recognize that a problem exists. In fact, they usually feel right about behaving the way they do, often to the point of believing they are perfectly well adjusted. People with personality disorders cannot see themselves as other people see them. Although they may be aware of and sometimes dissatisfied with the negative impact their behavior has on others, they are usually less aware that they are causing the problem. For that reason, families and friends of those with personality disorders can experience as much, if not more, distress as the disordered people themselves.

The term *personality disorder* may sound vaguely informal, but it actually encompasses a distinct category of behaviors as defined by the American Psychiatric Association's *Diagnostic and Statistical Manual of Mental Disorders* (third edition, revised 1987), commonly called the DSM-III. This is the standard reference work used by mental health professionals to diagnose mental illness. It includes virtually all known mental illnesses (about 230 are identified) and lists 11 different personality disorders, which are divided into 3 groups. The first group includes *paranoid, schizoid*, and *schizotypal* personality disorders. People with these disorders are often characterized as odd or eccentric. The second group includes *antisocial, borderline, histrionic*, and *narcissistic* personality disorders. These people often exhibit dramatic, emotional, or erratic behavior. The third group includes *avoidant, dependent, obsessive-compulsive*, and *passive-aggressive* personality disorders. People who suffer from these disorders frequently appear fearful and anxious.

Although there are no exact statistics, studies cited in the 1988 *New Harvard Guide to Psychiatry* have estimated that "15 percent of a general population can be expected to have personality disorders." And the *Comprehensive Textbook of Psychiatry* states, "No group of emotional disorders is more often encountered in psychiatric practice."

Everyone has probably come in contact with people who have one or more personality disorders. And even more frequently, everyone has encountered people who possess some of the traits found in those with personality disorders. Maladaptive traits such as exaggerated suspicion, rage-filled outbursts, or extreme self-centeredness, for example, are not hard to find in contemporary society. Most people may themselves, at one time or another, exhibit traits indicative of a personality disorder. However, the mere existence of these traits does not mean that a person has a personality disorder. Mental health practitioners must see the presence of several specific traits over a certain period of time, and they must rule out other diagnoses and explanations, before they will diagnose a personality disorder.

Most people with personality disorders, despite their inflexible and maladaptive behavior, somehow find a way to get by in the world. They develop their own unique ways of coping with life, ways that might not seem effective enough to others but that enable these people to meet their basic needs. A few such people with personality disorders even achieve great success, but they are the exception and not the rule.

Those with dependent personality disorder, for example, cope by submission. These people have an excessive dependency on others. They need constant reassurance and direction, even for making commonplace decisions such as which restaurant to eat in or what clothes to wear. They need a dominant person in their life, one who will make all the decisions. To ensure that such a person remains with them, dependent personalities constantly defer and demur, maintaining a fragile emotional balance by ingratiating themselves to others. Regrettably, such people often live in constant fear of being abandoned and left to fend for themselves. This self-defeating style also greatly inhibits initiative or achievement, both socially and professionally.

Even if people with personality disorders come to understand that their behavior is negative and self-defeating, they may not be able to change it easily. By the time a disordered individual reaches adulthood, maladaptive patterns are so firmly entrenched, so interwoven in the fabric of personality, that they appear almost automatically.

For example, a person with obsessive-compulsive personality disorder may come to realize that his or her exacting perfectionism interferes with completing work assignments on time but may not be able to resist the perfectionist impulse to set standards so high that nothing can ever meet them. Similarly, the person with borderline personality disorder may try to control his or her extreme mood swings but simply be unable to.

Within the wide spectrum of behavior that constitutes mental health on the one hand and serious mental illness on the other, personality disorders can be thought to occupy a kind of middle ground. People with personality disorders are not considered "normal," but neither are they considered as severely disturbed as those who suffer from *psychoses*, which are characterized by a complete break with reality. People with psychoses such as *schizophrenia*, a group of severe mental disorders, often cannot function in society and can be a threat to themselves and others. Most people with personality disorders manage to survive in the world, although often with little happiness.

It is important to realize that every "normal" person can experience moments or degrees of emotional behavior that are maladaptive and inflexible. There is no clear demarcation between normal and *pathological* (disease-causing) behavior. Many prominent characteristics of personality disorders—feeling anxious and fearful or being dramatic, emotional, or erratic—are relatively common. Most people, at one time or another, for example, have become suspicious that friends were talking about them behind their back. This does not necessarily indicate a paranoid personality disorder. A personality disorder occurs only when negative and maladaptive traits become so ingrained and so rigidly exercised that they begin to erode a person's mental health and successful ability to function.

The major distinction between a normal personality and a disordered personality is flexibility. A normally functioning person employs positive, adaptive coping strategies and learns from each new experience. If an impulsive and angry outburst at a teacher is punished by expulsion from school, most students learn to check their anger to avoid such punishment. Normal behavior is flexible enough to be modified. Those with personality disorders, unfortunately, are likely to repeat such outbursts—despite the consequences—because that maladaptive pattern is so ingrained.

People with personality disorders seem unable to learn new ways of behaving. In a sense, they are caught in a rut, compelled by habit to act in negative and inappropriate ways. And all too often, they do not recognize their actions as inappropriate. Faced with new situations, they fall back on old, maladaptive behaviors, unable to break out of the rut established early in their life.

WHAT CAUSES PERSONALITY DISORDERS?

Most psychiatrists and psychologists agree that disordered personalities have their roots in childhood and are the result of specific stresses in the environment. These stresses may be brought on by an unstable or unhappy home life, or they may simply stem from day-to-day life. To one degree or another, the stresses that underlie personality disorders are present in every person's life. Why do some people develop normally in the face of stress while others develop disorders?

There is no easy answer to that question. Just as there exists no exact line between normal and maladaptive behavior, there is no clear distinction between normal and maladaptive personality development. In some cases, it almost seems a matter of luck that one person develops normally while another with similar background and experiences does not.

It seems easier to understand why a neglected or physically abused child might develop a personality disorder more readily than a child from a so-called good home. And yet personality disorders affect people from all social and economic levels and from all walks of life, from the bleak inner city to the glitter of Hollywood to the mall life of suburbia. This raises the much-debated issue of *nature versus nurture*: Is heredity the major determinant in personality development, or is the environment—people, experiences, and conditions that surround someone—the most powerful force that shapes the way people act? Do people inherit their personalities, or do they learn them? Although research increasingly shows a strong correlation between heredity and personality, it is commonly accepted that both heredity and environment are essential elements of personality.

Most mental health professionals believe that personality disorders begin in childhood with attempts to cope with stress. These stresses may be either apparent, extreme stresses, such as child abuse or great poverty, or the more subtle day-to-day stresses that are part of every person's life. How an individual copes with stress may be related to his or her temperament.

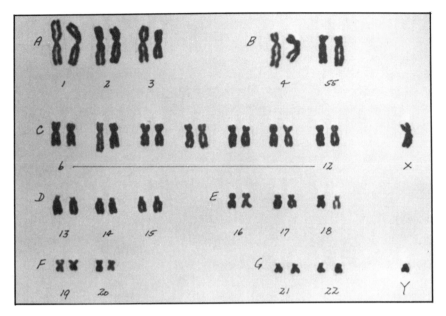

A karyotype shows the 23 pairs of chromosomes in a human cell. Research has shown a correlation between heredity and personality.

People are born with certain built-in inclinations, called *temperament*, that environment initially has nothing to do with. Temperament is often apparent from the moment of birth. Parents are amazed that one child will show a markedly different personality from his or her siblings. One infant might have a naturally pleasant disposition while another is irritable and cranky. One may sleep through the night while another is up at all hours.

Recent studies have also shown strong evidence that certain types of clinical depression, schizophrenia, and even alcoholism have strong genetic components. One does not necessarily inherit a gene for schizophrenia but may well inherit a *predisposition*, or susceptibility, to the disease. Although inheriting a disease is not the same as inheriting a personality, research suggests that genetics influences a great many aspects of a person's mental life and behavioral patterns.

At the same time, there is a great body of research strongly linking personality to environmental factors. The *behaviorist school*, a school of psychological thought established in the early

1900s, credits environmental factors with determining people's actions, feelings, and personality. People essentially learn personality by being rewarded or punished for their actions. A behavior is tried; if it is rewarded, or *positively reinforced*, it is likely to be repeated. If a particular behavior is punished or if the behavior does not end an unpleasant condition (*negative reinforcement*), it is less likely to be repeated. Eventually, traits are established based on the principles of reward and punishment. A young child need only touch a hot stove once to learn that such behavior is negatively reinforced—that is, with pain or a burn.

So, whereas heredity predisposes a person to certain behaviors, learned behavior dictates the degree to which those predispositions will develop. A child who is predisposed to a mental illness might not necessarily develop one, and certainly the lack of genetic predisposition is no guarantee of mental health. Personality development, whether normal or disordered, results from a complex interweaving of heredity and life experiences.

DIAGNOSING PERSONALITY DISORDERS

The significance of personality disorders within the overall framework of mental illness has only recently been recognized. Part of the reason is the relative prominence these disorders have gained in the DSM-III. Earlier editions did not clearly separate personality disorders from personality traits, and psychiatrists tended to diagnose personality disorders almost as a last resort. If a patient's problem was not severe enough to be diagnosed as a psychosis, it was often diagnosed as a *neurosis*, a term coined by Sigmund Freud, one of the founders of modern psychiatry, to describe maladaptive behavior motivated by unconscious, or repressed, anxiety. A personality disorder was rarely diagnosed.

There is a fundamental difference between neuroses and personality disorders. Neurotics suffer emotional pain. People with personality disorders often do not experience pain themselves but "act out" their emotional conflicts in behaviors that affect others. Because of this difference, neurotics seek out treatment and benefit from it more often than do people with personality disorders, who do not think there is anything terribly wrong with themselves. But, unlike neurotics, whose problems are generally limited to certain areas of functioning—a specific *phobia*, or ex-

Sigmund Freud, shown here, founded the field of psychoanalysis. Although many of his theories have fallen out of favor, he laid the groundwork for modern psychiatry.

aggerated fear, for example—personality disorders affect all areas of a person's life. As personality disorders are better understood and diagnostic methods are expanded and refined, it becomes more apparent that these disorders affect a large number of people.

The development of personality, normal and disordered, is unique to every individual. But by systematically classifying personality disorders and by listing symptoms, associated disorders, and other pertinent information, the DSM-III and other diagnostic resources provide a valuable tool for psychiatrists, psychologists, counselors, and social workers who treat and care for those with disordered personalities.

Some medical authorities take exception to the DSM-III's approach because it too readily allows people to be categorized and because many of the personality disorders are hard to define and overlap with other disorders. But classification is widely seen as an important step in the basic understanding and subsequent treatment of personality disorders. Labeling patients can have negative effects, however. Rightly or wrongly, people can be pigeonholed into certain categories, which may complicate successful treatment.

Diagnoses of mental illness must be made with great care. But no matter how scrupulous the care taken in diagnosing patients, psychiatry and psychology are still inexact sciences, and the human mind is so complex that incorrect diagnoses cannot be completely eliminated. Significant advances are being made in

Diagnosing personality disorders is difficult because the symptoms of these disorders often overlap and because the patients may be uncooperative, feeling that they do not actually have a problem.

the treatment of mental illnesses, but personality disorders remain extremely difficult to identify and treat.

Diagnosis is difficult because symptoms of one personality disorder are likely to appear with other disorders. Treatment is difficult because those with personality disorders seldom think they have a problem. Such people are reluctant to seek out professional help and are usually uncooperative when forced to do so. This places an added strain on family members and professional care givers. As the following chapters of this volume attest, the maladaptive patterns of the disordered personality, established and reinforced in the earliest years of life, are extremely difficult to reverse.

•   •   •   •

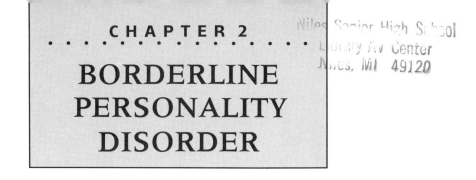

BORDERLINE PERSONALITY DISORDER

Rage, *Michelangelo (1475–1564)*

The DSM-III defines borderline personality disorder as a "pervasive pattern of instability of self-image, interpersonal relationships, and mood." Borderline personality disorder is one of the most serious, confounding, and controversial of all the personality disorders. It is serious because those with this disorder are prone to explosive, violent, and sometimes suicidal behavior. It is confounding because so many of its symptoms occur with other disorders that it is sometimes hard to make an accurate diagnosis. It is controversial because of its very name.

25

In the early 1900s, the term *borderline* was used to describe patients whose symptoms fell somewhere between neurosis and psychosis and bordered on many different disorders. Later, the term *ambulatory schizophrenia* was used to describe the same basic symptoms, and for many years borderline personality disorder was actually thought to be a mild type of schizophrenia.

Borderlines can and do experience brief *psychotic episodes*, periods during which there is a break with reality, but today the consensus is that borderline personality disorder is not a form of schizophrenia. Many mental health professionals believe the word *borderline* is too vague and inexact to adequately describe this puzzling disorder.

Studies from the *New Harvard Guide to Psychiatry* estimate that between 15% and 25% of all hospitalized psychiatric patients, as well as perhaps 4% of the general population, suffer from borderline personality disorder. Almost three times as many women as men suffer from this disorder.

Interestingly, because many borderline characteristics—lack of identity, impulsive behavior, extreme mood swings—are a relatively normal part of adolescence, it is difficult to accurately diagnose borderline personality disorder until after the age of 16, when more stable patterns of behavior are developed.

Because of what psychoanalyst James F. Masterson, professor of clinical psychiatry at Cornell University Medical College, has called a "deficient emotional investment in the self," those with borderline personalities have very unstable identities. They are uncertain about such things as which types of friends to choose and which set of values to embrace. They show confusion about sexual orientation, career goals, and other long-range plans.

Interpersonal relationships are equally unstable and marked by great intensity, alternating from *overidealization* to *devaluation*. These two terms refer to a kind of love-hate cycle in which the borderline can view an intimate friend or family member as wonderful one moment and wicked the next. With the borderline, everything is perceived as either all good or all bad; there is little room for anything between.

Borderline behavior regularly swings from obliging dependency to angry self-assertiveness. Within moments, a person's mood can shift unpredictably from depression to elation, from irritability and anxiety to outright violence. These mood swings, which generally last only a few hours and seldom more than a few days, can be triggered by events such as real or perceived criticism or fear of abandonment, but they can be caused by almost anything.

Borderline personalities exhibit a great deal of *behavioral dyscontrol*, that is, they have difficulty restraining their impulses. As a result, they often engage in self-defeating behavior. Many borderlines are sexually promiscuous; embark on eating binges or shopping sprees; and are prone to compulsive gambling or drug and alcohol abuse. Not surprisingly, these problems often cause other mental and physical difficulties beyond the *primary symptoms*, or those initially connected with the disorder.

One patient in her thirties, who for years had no idea she had a borderline personality disorder, was perplexed by her inability to control her drinking or maintain a long-term relationship with a man. Her relationships always ended badly, often with violence. It was as if her life were one vicious cycle, wildly fluctuating between the highest highs and the lowest lows, and she was helpless to do anything about it.

People with borderline personality disorder have trouble exerting control over their impulses. They may engage in compulsive gambling or other activities that are self-defeating.

Recurrent threats of or attempts at suicide and self-mutilating behavior are serious symptoms of borderline personality disorder. When they do not prove fatal, such behaviors actually seem to calm the rage experienced by these people.

As with all personality disorders, stress is an important factor in the onset of maladaptive behavior. In the case of the borderline personality, stress triggers *dysphoria*, a combination of anxiety, depression, and anger that can rapidly intensify. The borderline's impulsive and explosive behavior is a strategy to combat the trauma of dysphoria.

"There is a propensity to act in ways that relieve the inner state of distress," says Rex W. Cowdry, clinical director of the National Institute of Mental Health, in a recently published interview. "These individuals tend towards self-injury, or to knocking themselves out with alcohol or drugs. . . . The other major type of behavioral dyscontrol involves rage episodes, which are a hallmark, indeed one of the diagnostic criteria, of borderline personality disorder."

Rage can manifest itself in several ways—physical violence directed toward friends or family, self-mutilation, or actual suicide attempts. Wrist slashing and recurrent suicide threats are all-too-common patterns for the borderline. Patients interviewed for a National Institute of Mental Health study told of actually carving words in their skin, scraping sandpaper across their face, and in one case, puncturing an eardrum.

Oddly, this self-mutilating behavior appears to calm the rage that has welled up from within, and borderline patients have reported being relieved of dysphoria in that manner. Unfortunately, many borderlines develop *major depression*, a serious and long-lasting type of depression, as a result of their illness, placing them at greater risk for actual suicide attempts, which may prove successful.

In the absence of stress, the borderline's symptoms are usually unremarkable. In other words, the person might appear relatively normal. Yet, even during stable periods, borderlines report a deep-seated feeling of anger and depression and often chronic, or long-standing, feelings of emptiness.

Another key feature of borderline personality disorder is a fear of being alone. Most borderlines will go out of their way, sometimes frantically, to avoid being abandoned by the people near them. Ironically, because they sometimes feel forced into dependent situations, they can also lash out at the very people they cling to.

CAUSES

The lack of identity that is thought to cause the ambivalent emotions typical of borderline personality disorder is likely the product of early childhood stress and anxiety. According to one theory, developed in the early 1970s by Otto F. Kernberg, now a professor of psychiatry at Cornell University Medical College, the developing infant comes to perceive the mother in two distinct ways: on the one hand, as a loving, nurturing person who provides security and closeness; on the other, as a punishing, neglectful mother who often abandons the child for no reason and fails to meet the infant's emotional needs. "This ambivalent view of the mother," according to the *Comprehensive Textbook of Psychiatry*, "is intensely anxiety producing in the child, since both mothers are the same person on whom he is dependent. In theory, the defense of splitting is deployed to keep these separate experiences apart; otherwise anxiety would continually overwhelm the infant." Splitting is a *defense mechanism*, an involuntary process that tries to relieve conflict and anxiety, by which the individual compartmentalizes, or splits, feelings into distinct categories. In the adult borderline, this defense mechanism translates into the perception of individuals as either all good or all bad.

Normally, infants learn to enjoy strong bonds with parents and also—with the parents' help—to become independent individuals. However, when parents do not, or cannot, allow this separateness to occur, the resulting anxiety and lack of identity can eventually lead to borderline personality disorder.

Many researchers believe that there may be a genetic predisposition to borderline personality disorder because not all children who grow up in such emotionally unstable environments develop the disorder. Although there is currently no convincing proof of such a genetic link, studies of borderlines have shown that in roughly 2% to 4% of cases, borderlines' relatives also had the disorder.

Borderlines often come from emotionally impoverished backgrounds. Histories of abuse, incest, violence, and alcoholism are commonly reported, as are traumatic family breakups, adoptions, and separations in infancy and early childhood.

Norma Jean Baker was raised under many of these conditions. Illegitimate, she never knew her father. When she was a child, her mother was institutionalized for depression, and Norma Jean, who would later become one of the greatest Hollywood sex symbols of her era as Marilyn Monroe, spent most of her childhood in and out of foster homes. "The whole world around me just crumbled," she recalled of her childhood.

Apart from her tremendous fame, Marilyn Monroe's tragic life (she apparently committed suicide at the age of 36) can be seen as a fairly typical example of the borderline personality syndrome. From the emotional trauma of her childhood came the later manifestations: a weak sense of self; a series of self-defeating and short-lived relationships with men, beginning with an impulsive marriage at the age of 16; promiscuity; drug and alcohol abuse; a fear of abandonment; depression; and an emotional instability that toward the end of her life branded her among Hollywood producers as unemployable. "To put it bluntly," Marilyn said shortly before her death in 1962, "I seem to be a whole superstructure with no foundation."

Author Gloria Steinem writes in her book *Marilyn*:

> Emotional security, continuity, a sense of being loved unconditionally for oneself—all those turn out to be as important to a child's development as all but the

Marilyn Monroe is believed to have suffered from borderline personality disorder. She exhibited many of the self-defeating and impulsive behaviors connected with the disorder.

most basic food and shelter. It was exactly these emotional basics that Norma Jean lacked. And she was deprived of them in the earliest years of her life, when the resulting damage to a sense of self is most difficult to repair.

Marilyn Monroe also shared another trait common to many borderlines: creative ability. "One of the striking things about many borderline individuals is that they have an intriguing degree of creativity," Cowdry has written, "a readier access to intuitions and feeling states. If they are not overwhelming, those states can actually be beneficial. . . . It's hard to turn the liability of the disorder into an asset, but it can be done in some cases."

DIAGNOSIS AND TREATMENT

There are a range of overlapping symptoms from other disorders commonly associated with borderline personality disorder. "Frequently," states the DSM-III, "this disorder is accompanied by many features of other personality disorders, such as schizotypal, histrionic, narcissistic, and antisocial personality disorders. In many cases more than one diagnosis is warranted."

Overlapping symptoms can make both diagnosis and treatment of the borderline patient a difficult task. Is there any hope, then, for people suffering from this disorder? The answer appears to be a cautious yes. Although there is no cure for the disorder, the intensity of the symptoms appears to diminish with age. Borderlines experience their most severe symptoms in their twenties and thirties. As they get older, it appears easier for them to manage emotional swings. Psychiatrists and psychologists report seeing few severe borderline patients in their forties or older.

Currently, the most successful treatment for borderline disorder seems to be psychotherapy. With the help of a therapist, borderline patients can analyze their emotional life, determine the causes of repressed anxiety and trauma, and, by gaining insights into these unresolved inner conflicts, come to a greater understanding of the disorder itself and how they are affected by it.

Some therapists try to teach a therapeutic technique called *reflective delay*, an approach aimed at combating dysphoria and explosive behavior through reasoning. "It's that process," Cowdry explains, "of anticipating problems, of identifying problems when they arise, connecting them with events, and charting courses of action using ego strengths—that is at the heart of the treatment of borderline personality disorder."

Several drug therapies have also been employed to reduce anxiety, depression, and violent behavior in those with borderline personality disorder, but as yet there is no standard drug treatment for the disorder. Each case must be treated individually, especially in light of overlapping and associated disorders. Drug therapies and other treatment approaches for the personality disorders are discussed in greater detail in Chapter 8.

As is all too often the case, however, many people with borderline personality disorder fail to recognize their condition and therefore never seek professional help. They continue to be trapped on an emotional roller coaster, bewildered and depressed by their explosive and unpredictable behavior, one moment clinging to friends and loved ones, lashing out at them the next.

•　　　•　　　•　　　•

CHAPTER 3

ANTISOCIAL PERSONALITY DISORDER

I magine living entirely in a cold, heartless world where everyone is conniving and suspicious, power over others is the overriding measure of success, cruelty and abuse are accepted facts of life, and the proverbial nice guy does indeed finish last. This is the world as perceived by someone with an antisocial personality disorder.

Given such a dismal and threatening perspective, full of deep-seated hostility and mistrust, it is no wonder that people with antisocial personality disorder play out their life against a backdrop of aggression and uncaring manipulation. To their way of thinking, such aggressive and often illegal behavior is simply the only way to deal with this sort of world.

Antisocial personality disorder is characterized by an ingrained pattern of irresponsible and antisocial behavior, behavior that goes against society's norms. Individuals with this disorder are extremely aggressive, competitive, quick to argue, and quick to anger. They have a need to exert control over their environment and the people in it and are usually impulsive risk takers and thrill seekers, often to the point of recklessness.

Although many with this disorder have developed a practiced geniality—even, in some cases, a remarkable ability to charm and seemingly befriend others—beneath this affable mask is a calculating manipulator who cares little for anyone else's welfare and who is highly mistrusting of almost everyone.

One of the most striking features about people with antisocial personality disorder is a lack of guilt, anxiety, or remorse for their actions. These people do not seem to have a conscience. They do not adhere to accepted principles of right and wrong because to them the world is a harsh, ruthless place and to manage in it one must be just as harsh and ruthless. Antisocial personalities may even feel justified in hurting or mistreating others and often take a perverse pleasure in the inflated sense of power it gives them.

As a result, says the DSM-III, antisocial personality disorder "is often extremely incapacitating, resulting in failure to become an independent, self-supporting adult and giving rise to many years of institutionalization, more commonly penal than mental." The DSM-III also notes that people with antisocial personality disorder "are more likely than people in the general population to die prematurely by violent means."

Unable to delay the gratification of desires like most normally adjusted people, the antisocial personality continually acts in impulsive, aggressive, and often illegal ways to get what he or she wants, displaying a flagrant disregard for authority, rules, or the rights of others.

People with antisocial personality disorder, who are sometimes referred to as *psychopaths* or *sociopaths*, are commonly found among those involved in criminal activity. Estimates are that perhaps as many as 75% of all imprisoned criminals have antisocial personalities. But it is not only criminals who have this disorder. It is believed that in the general population about 3% of American men and 1% of American women are affected.

"In its mildest forms," writes psychiatrist Theodore Millon,

> the antisocial personality, as a rule, frequently fits into the mainstream of our society. These milder manifestations are often not only commended, but they are endorsed and cultivated in our competitive society where tough, hardheaded realism is an admired attribute. Such personality characteristics are often considered necessary for survival in the cold, cruel business world, in political arenas, and in military and quasi-military organizations, such as police departments.

An extreme example of a society so skewed that even a seriously antisocial person could succeed was Nazi Germany. Field Marshall Hermann Göring, one of Adolf Hitler's top commanders

Field Marshal Hermann Göring is thought to have suffered from antisocial personality disorder. He was a daring air force flyer during World War I and was known for his brutal, sometimes bizarre behavior.

during World War II, was such a person. Göring, who reportedly told his troops, "Shoot first and ask questions later," admitted that he felt no guilt or remorse about creating the German concentration camps during the war that resulted in the death of 6 million Jews.

Like other antisocial personalities, Göring was a risk taker and thrill seeker, a daring flyer in the air force who seemed to crave high levels of stimulation. Also like other antisocial personalities, he was unable to delay gratification of his desires. Göring was "a gargantuan eater and drinker," according to C. S. Bluemel. Although he could be personable and of good cheer, displaying the same cordial mask as many antisocial personalities, Göring was also unscrupulous and callous to the feelings of others. Iron Hermann, as he was called, took great pleasure in mortifying guests at his estate. Worse still, there were countless people put to death on Göring's order, prompting the bizarre but nonetheless accurate description of him as "an affable, hearty butcher."

Details of Göring's childhood and what effect they may have had on his later life are unclear, but in the majority of antisocial personality cases, symptoms are recognizable early on. Both in childhood and adolescence, the disorder manifests itself in lying, cheating, stealing, vandalism, fighting, physical cruelty, truancy from school, boredom with repetitive tasks, and an early, aggressive interest in sexual activity. In adulthood, reckless and impulsive behavior continues and may lead to drug and alcohol use, promiscuity, child and spouse abuse, failure to honor financial obligations, and a range of criminal behaviors from petty theft and forgery to rape and murder.

With few exceptions, antisocial personalities are raised in homes devoid of warmth, love, and trust. They fail to develop the close emotional ties characteristic of a normally developed personality and instead learn to be angry and hostile. The child who will grow up to have an antisocial personality disorder learns early in life to be hard hearted and emotionally self-reliant and to trust no one.

Considering their deep-seated hostility and mistrust toward virtually everyone, it is not surprising that personal relationships turn out badly for those with antisocial personality disorder. Manipulative, with little regard for the feelings of others, the antisocial person can only think of, or care about, him- or herself, not the consequences his or her behavior will have on others.

In one study of psychopathic behavior, a 30-year-old man recently released from prison for fraud, bigamy, and other crimes, told of a childhood of lying, cheating, bullying, and theft. As an adolescent, he was involved in drugs and alcohol, as well as in crimes such as forgery. At the age of 22, he impulsively married a woman almost twice his age who supported him financially. Other marriages followed. When he was tired or bored, the man would simply leave his wife of several months, travel elsewhere, and take up with another woman. When interviewed, he voiced no remorse for his actions. He felt his behavior had been justified as a practical way of getting along in the world.

Many people with antisocial personality disorder get into trouble with the law, but having this disorder does not mean that one will exhibit criminal behavior. The mean-spirited boss who seems to delight in belittling employees and who never admits to being wrong; the manipulative politician who will say anything, true or false, to gain power over others; the overzealous police officer who seems to enjoy using force to subdue suspects; or the con artist who will cheat and lie to satisfy his or her needs with no regard for his or her so-called friends—all these types fit the profile of the antisocial personality, and all are common in today's society.

CAUSES AND TREATMENTS

There is no consensus as to what causes antisocial personality disorder; the debate between nature and nurture—heredity and environment—is a spirited one. In recent years, however, studies have suggested a strong genetic link for the disorder, particularly between fathers and their male offspring.

Having a sociopathic or alcoholic father is a powerful indicator that a male offspring will develop antisocial personality disorder, even if the child is not raised in the same household as the father. Statistically, reports the DSM-III, "antisocial personality disorder is five times more common among first-degree biologic relatives of males with the disorder than among the general population."

There is also a very high incidence of alcoholism among individuals with antisocial personality disorder, complicating a clear-cut diagnosis. In some individuals, alcoholism is a reflection of an antisocial personality disorder, probably linked to the inability to control impulses. But alcoholism also is sometimes a symptom of underlying depression, and other times it seems to stem from environmental factors. Not everyone with antisocial personality disorder is an alcoholic, and not all alcoholics have an antisocial personality disorder.

Other studies have shown that the *autonomic nervous system*, that part of the nervous system that governs involuntary actions such as breathing and blinking, generates particularly weak responses to sensory stimulation in those with antisocial personality disorder. This suggests that antisocial personalities are relatively numb to sensory stimulation. If that is the case, the risk taking and thrill seeking common to the disorder might be explained as an attempt to increase sensory stimulation.

It has been further theorized that a weak autonomic nervous system response may also inhibit internal feelings of pain, anxiety, or guilt, which could explain why the antisocial person lacks a sense of right or wrong and feels no remorse for hurting and abusing others.

Additional research focusing on brain chemistry suggests that antisocial personalities, particularly psychopathic killers, may have in common a short supply of *serotonin*. Serotonin is one of a group of chemicals in the brain and nervous system that carry nerve impulses across the *synapses*, or spaces, between brain or nerve cells. These chemicals are called *neurotransmitters*. Serotonin is believed to play a role in regulating sleep and emotional behavior. Researchers believe that low levels of serotonin—possibly an inherited deficiency—might trigger the impulsive violence and aggression that are trademarks of antisocial personality disorder. Studies of antisocial prisoners have shown low levels of serotonin by-products in spinal fluid. Other studies have consistently shown lower levels of serotonin by-products in depressed patients who attempted suicide. The message appears to be that low serotonin levels are associated with the impulsive behavior that encourages depressed people to attempt suicide; low serotonin may also be associated with the impulsive activity of antisocial individuals. The major antidepressant drugs act by elevating the levels of serotonin at synapses in the brain.

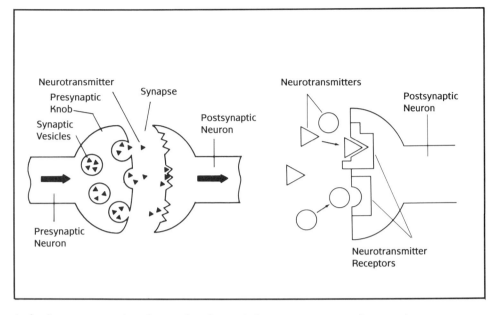

Left: *One neuron signals another by emitting a neurotransmitter such as serotonin across a synapse.* Right: *Each neurotransmitter fits one kind of receptor on the target neuron. Low levels of serotonin are thought to be connected to the lack of impulse control exhibited by those with anti-social personality disorder.*

There is little doubt that environmental factors are also important. It has already been shown how cultural circumstances can reinforce antisocial behavior, as was the case with Hermann Göring in Nazi Germany and to a lesser extent in today's often cold and insensitive business and political arenas.

Behaviorists, who believe that people learn to act the way they do by trial-and-error testing of successful behavior, point out that antisocial personalities often have antisocial fathers whose behavior is observed and mimicked by the child. Other studies suggest that the acute mistrust and hostility common to those with antisocial personality disorder have their roots in maternal deprivation or parental hostility during the first years of life. Still other theories suggest that inconsistent discipline by parents allows children to grow up without a clear understanding of right and wrong, thus aiding in the development of the disorder.

Without the benefits of such emotions as warmth and tenderness, antisocial personalities learn to mistrust others and become excellent deceivers and manipulators. As Millon writes, "Unconstrained by honesty and truth, they weave impressive tales of competency and reliability. Many are disarmingly charming in initial encounters and become skillful swindlers and impostors. Alert to weakness in others, they play their games of deception with considerable skill."

It is precisely for this reason—the ease with which antisocial personalities can adopt a mask of charm and sincerity—that treatment of the adult antisocial personality can be a frustrating and frequently unsuccessful undertaking. Those with antisocial personality disorder are so mistrustful of others, particularly authority figures such as psychiatrists or therapists, that they seldom cooperate. Moreover, they rarely believe they themselves are to blame for their actions.

During the past 50 years, there has been a revolution in drug therapy for the treatment of mental disorders, but as yet there is no consistently successful drug for treating antisocial personality disorder. The best approach, one being used most in prisons and other institutional settings, appears to consist of various forms of group counseling, the so-called talking therapies.

It has been observed that when antisocial people are forced into a counseling situation with their peers, they can discover common experiences, frustrations, and difficulties that will make them aware of their illness. The critical factor in successfully treating this disorder is making antisocial people aware that they are responsible for their own actions.

Realistically, however, current treatment methods offer little cause for enthusiasm. As with other personality disorders, though, time appears to help alleviate the more severe symptoms. Much like borderline disorder, antisocial symptoms reach their peak in the twenties. In many cases, as the disordered individual reaches his or her thirties and forties, symptoms such as violent behavior tend to diminish.

•   •   •   •

CHAPTER 4

HISTRIONIC AND NARCISSISTIC PERSONALITY DISORDERS

Mask with Small Flag, *Paul Klee*
(1879–1940)

Histrionic and narcissistic personality disorders are frequently associated with each other because people with these disorders exhibit similar patterns of dramatic and emotional behavior and because these people have an almost insatiable need for approval from others. It is natural for people to seek recognition from friends and from those whom they admire, but in the case of histrionic and narcissistic personalities, the need for attention and approval can become all-consuming.

These people will go to great lengths to make others believe they are special. But in the process, they rely on self-defeating behaviors that are exploitative, manipulative, and show a profound lack of *empathy*, that is, understanding or sensitivity, for the needs and desires of others.

Histrionics and narcissists constantly advertise their "specialness" to others. However, they are not usually what they appear to be. They may put on a front of warmth and sincerity or of cool self-reliance, but behind that facade is the true self—one that craves attention and approval and has little consideration for others. Histrionics and narcissists need attention and approval to bolster a weak self-image. They feel special only when others say that they are, so they adopt an image that they think will make them appear unique. Unfortunately, in their attempt to gain recognition and approval, they hide their real self, not only from others, but also from themselves. As a result, histrionics and narcissists know very little about what motivates their behavior or how they are really viewed by others.

HISTRIONIC PERSONALITY DISORDER

In a classroom, at a party, or at some other gathering, there is frequently one person who is the center of attention, seeming to

Exhibiting attention-getting behavior on occasion is normal, but when it becomes intense and constant it may be a sign of histrionic personality disorder and may be a cover for a weak self-image.

bask in the glow of celebrity. Often this person is physically attractive, flirtatious, and given to provocative and seductive dress. His or her actions and mannerisms in the presence of others suggests a kind of emotional theatricality, almost a stage performance. These people are always "on." Under normal circumstances, there are many positive traits associated with such a sociable personality type. People with these characteristics can be outgoing, energetic, charming, and able to form friendships easily with a wide variety of people.

For those with histrionic personality disorder, such sociable behavior is carried to extremes. People with this disorder display a pattern of excessive emotionality, and although it is true they make friends easily, their friendships are usually short-lived.

After a friendship has lasted for a while, histrionics will invariably begin to act manipulatively, and their apparent sincerity will be seen by friends as shallow and superficial. Histrionics are not really interested in others, only the approval others are able to bestow. Eventually, the histrionic person will come to be seen by his or her peers as conceited and insincere.

Because people with histrionic personality disorder are so busy performing for attention and approval, they rarely see themselves as others see them. The term *histrionic* refers to overacting, being artificial, or showing affected behavior. "Emotions are often expressed with inappropriate exaggeration," the DSM-III states.

> For example, the person may appear to be much more sad, angry, or delighted than would seem to be warranted. People with this disorder tend to be very self-centered, with little or no tolerance for the frustration of delayed gratification. Their actions are directed to obtaining immediate satisfaction.

The case study of a 34-year-old woman named Suzanne is in many ways typical. Suzanne sought treatment because her third marriage was falling apart. Although she had a good relationship with her current husband, was financially secure, and had virtually unlimited freedom to pursue her interests, Suzanne felt the need to flirt with other men and to have affairs. This pattern had been established in her previous two marriages, and she had only vague ideas about why she did it or how to control it.

As a child, Suzanne said, she felt forced to compete with her sister for their parents' attention and approval. She was attractive and outgoing, popular in high school, had many dates, and was emotionally well adjusted. In her marriages, however, she quickly became bored and felt the need to seek attention from other men. She would flirt, dress suggestively, and eventually have affairs. Her need for attention and approval was never satisfied, and the maladaptive pattern was wreaking havoc on her life.

Suzanne's story illustrates the histrionic's need for excitement and new experiences. People with histrionic personality disorder are highly impressionable as well, more willing than most to adopt the latest fad or to embrace strong authority figures who might hold the key to their happiness. Such shallow emotions and a weak self-image make for a personality easily influenced by the opinions of others and overly concerned with physical attractiveness and looking youthful.

Although peers eventually see through the shallowness and superficiality, most histrionic personalities would probably describe themselves as warm and gregarious. That is because they lack the ability for introspection and use defense mechanisms such as *dissociation* and *repression* to mask their true self.

Dissociation is a defense mechanism in which a person temporarily alters or separates part of his or her identity or personality, in a sense, splitting the "true self" from the "false self." In the histrionic's case, this true self is always kept hidden. Repression is another defense mechanism in which people unconsciously push negative events and disturbing wishes and emotions to the far corners of their mind, becoming unable to remember them consciously. Dissociation and repression are ways in which histrionic personalities avoid the pain of dealing with their maladaptive behavior and their fragile self-image.

Causes

Although little research is available to pinpoint the causes of histrionic personality disorder, it is believed they are similar to those found in many of the other personality disorders. Genetic

During the late 19th century, women were frequently diagnosed as hysterics for a range of behaviors thought to be common to their sex. Histrionic personality disorder has its roots in, but is quite different from, the Victorian conception of hysteria.

predispositions notwithstanding, physically and emotionally neglected children or those exposed to extreme stress or trauma at a young age seem to be at high risk.

Some researchers believe histrionic disorder is caused by parents who place exaggerated importance on so-called performance behavior. For example, a parent might only give praise when the child plays the piano for guests or is dressed up for a special occasion. Thus, the child learns to perform to gain approval and becomes dependent on others for self-esteem.

The term *histrionic personality disorder* evolved from the words *hysterical personality* and from *hysteria* before that. The term *hysteria* comes from the Latin word for uterus. Hysterical behavior, characterized by wild excitability and excessive anxiety, was originally believed to stem from dysfunction of the female gonads. Hysteria is one of the oldest diagnoses in the field of mental illness. In the late 1800s, during the repressive Victorian era, hysteria was regularly diagnosed to describe maladies thought to be common in women. This diagnosis is more correctly given to those with physical symptoms, usually associated with voluntary muscles of the body (such as the inability to move an arm or leg), that can be shown to have an emotional source.

Histrionic personality disorder is different from the original concept of hysteria, but even so, the disorder is still found overwhelmingly in women, which has led some to conclude that *sex bias* plays a role in the diagnosis. If women have been traditionally viewed by men as excitable, emotional, and prone to seeking attention and if men still make up the majority of the practitioners who diagnose mental illnesses, the predominance of histrionic personality disorder in women could well reflect male bias. Some mental health professionals think that men who show hysterical symptoms are less often diagnosed as histrionic than are women with the same symptoms. It is also likely that gender bias in society and the ways in which female children have traditionally been socialized predispose more women than men to develop histrionic personality disorder.

Treatment

Treating histrionic personality disorder is a difficult task. Currently, no *pharmacological*, that is drug or chemical, treatment is thought to be beneficial. The best treatment approach appears to be an ongoing program of psychotherapy in which patients are helped to find the true self they have for so long hidden behind a facade of warmth and gregariousness. Therapy is also considered appropriate for treating narcissistic personality disorder. Both of these disorders have yet to be thoroughly studied to determine more specific causes and treatments.

NARCISSISTIC PERSONALITY DISORDER

People with narcissistic personality disorder are exploitative—like those with histrionic personality disorder, who exploit others to maintain their fragile sense of self-esteem—but they use different tactics to achieve their goals. The histrionic is likely to be warm and sociable; the narcissist appears cool and aloof.

The term *narcissism* comes from Greek mythology. Narcissus was a Grecian youth possessed of amazing beauty. One day, by chance, he gazed upon himself in the reflection of a pool of water and fell instantly in love with his image. He was so smitten he refused to move and eventually died where he stood. Upon his death, the legend says, he turned into a flower—the narcissus.

Like Narcissus, people with narcissistic personality disorder are smitten with an inflated image of themselves. They are extremely self-centered and display an excessive sense of self-importance. They have grandiose fantasies of unlimited success that carry over into their behavior. Narcissists believe they are special and deserve special treatment from those around them. "They tend to exaggerate their accomplishments and talents," notes the DSM-III, "and expect to be noticed as 'special' even without appropriate achievement. They often feel that because of their 'specialness,' their problems are unique, and can be understood only by other special people."

The idea of narcissism is based on a Greek myth about a youth, Narcissus, who fell in love with his own image. Those with narcissistic personality disorder display an exaggerated sense of self-esteem but often only to disguise their weak self-image.

Technically, narcissism can be defined as self-love, and by itself self-love is not a bad thing. But those with narcissistic personality disorder have fallen in love with an image, not with their true self. They idealize a facade, one they have painstakingly created. This discrepancy between the true self and the superficial self can cause a great deal of anxiety.

"People with narcissistic personality disorder have severe problems maintaining a realistic concept of their own worth," states Robert J. Waldinger in his book *Fundamentals of Psychiatry*. "They generally set goals and make demands of themselves that are utterly unrealistic, and then feel inadequate and helpless when they fail to meet these standards."

Narcissists act as if they feel a sense of entitlement, believing that they deserve respect and special treatment from others, regardless of whether they have actually earned it. For example, narcissists might not like to wait in lines like "regular" people, or they might flagrantly disobey traffic signs or speed limits, believing that such rules do not apply to them. And like histrionics, narcissists show an extreme lack of empathy for the feelings of others. But, although narcissists present themselves as special, the slightest criticism from others, either real or perceived, can result in humiliation and rage and can make them feel acutely unworthy. Deep inside, narcissists do not think they are better than everyone else; they are intrinsically quite insecure. As stated in the DSM-III, "self-esteem is almost invariably very fragile."

One 36-year-old man with narcissistic personality disorder was stunned to find out that his wife of 12 years was going to divorce him. He was also shocked to learn that she had had a series of affairs during their marriage, largely because of his preoccupation with himself and his lack of involvement with her. In therapy, the man admitted being selfishly involved with his own interests and oblivious to the needs of his wife and children, but he had not realized it until his wife and others pointed it out. And by then it was too late.

In their relationships with others, narcissists can not only be selfish and insensitive but also envious. They have constant fantasies of power, wealth, and success and can experience tremendous envy toward those who have achieved successes greater than their own. Many narcissists are successful at jobs and careers,

Some professionals believe that a grandiose sense of self is a normal part of childhood but feel that those with narcissistic personality disorder never outgrow this attitude.

but because they are usually driven in their pursuit of success, it affords them only minimal satisfaction once attained.

Narcissists also pride themselves on self-reliance. This sets them apart from histrionic people, who are largely and obviously dependent on others for approval and recognition. Narcissists also crave admiration and attention, but they act as if such admiration is due them without effort. Narcissists look down on dependence as a sign of weakness.

Causes

Although narcissistic symptoms are rarely seen until adulthood, it is assumed that the narcissist's pathological overinvestment in self begins in childhood. Some theories say that a grandiose sense of self is a normal part of every child's personality development and that this normal pattern is somehow arrested in the narcissistic personality.

Other theories suggest that inadequate parenting may be partially responsible for the disorder. Parents who fail to appropriately value youthful assertiveness or who fail to help children take pride in their accomplishments, for example, may aid in the development of the disorder. This might explain why narcissists grow up with such an unsteady sense of self and need to be thought of as special by those around them.

Unfortunately, as with histrionic disorder, little is actually known about the exact causes of narcissistic personality disorder. Furthermore, because narcissistic characteristics are common in many other personality disorders, some psychiatrists and psychologists have questioned whether narcissism should be a separate diagnostic category or simply be incorporated into other disorders.

• • • •

CHAPTER 5

PARANOID, SCHIZOID, AND SCHIZOTYPAL PERSONALITY DISORDERS

Delusions of grandeur

To properly understand paranoid, schizoid, and schizotypal personality disorders, it is first necessary to know something about the more serious disorder schizophrenia.

Schizophrenia is a devastating brain disease characterized by psychotic behavior. Victims experience *delusions*, or persistent false beliefs not shared by others; *hallucinations*, or perceptions having no basis in reality; and severely disordered ways of thinking, speaking, and acting. When most people think of madness or insanity, schizophrenia is probably what comes to mind. Schizophrenics may babble incoherently, jumping from one subject to another, making up words as they go. They may spin extraordinary tales of persecution, saying that they are being sought by the FBI or the KGB. They might claim to be a king, a president, or even God.

Schizophrenics often dress oddly, appearing disheveled and unkempt. Around other people, they may be eccentric, extremely nervous, or totally detached. Faced with the news that a family member has just died, the schizophrenic might show no emotion at all or begin to laugh uncontrollably.

No one knows exactly what causes this crippling illness, only that it is widespread. Each year, 100,000 Americans are newly diagnosed as schizophrenics, and the estimated cost to society—for hospitalization, disability and welfare payments, lost wages, and treatment—is a staggering $10 billion to $20 billion annually.

The term *schizophrenia* has in recent years come to represent not one but a number of similar disorders. There are subtypes of the disease, as well as other mental illnesses that include schizophrenia-like symptoms.

People with paranoid, schizoid, and schizotypal personality disorders, for example, exhibit many schizophrenic behaviors, but they are less severe than the symptoms shown by actual schizophrenics. People with these personality disorders are not schizophrenic. Instead, they are said to fall within the so-called healthy end of the schizophrenic spectrum.

Occasionally, people with paranoid, schizoid, and schizotypal personality disorders might experience psychotic episodes, but these are usually brief and are not typical. The person with a paranoid personality disorder may, from time to time, believe that he or she is being spied upon. But the true paranoid schizophrenic has fixed delusions, perhaps that the CIA has been on his or her trail for many years.

People with paranoid, schizoid, and schizotypal personalities may appear odd, eccentric, and emotionally withdrawn. In social situations they may be extremely anxious or detached, or display unusual patterns of speech or ideas. Still, although such symptoms resemble schizophrenia, they are not severe enough to warrant the actual diagnosis of schizophrenia.

Although paranoid, schizoid, and schizotypal personality disorders can be serious in their own right, people with these disorders seldom require institutionalization and rarely seek treatment. Whereas they may suffer hardships at work, their major difficulties lie with social interaction and interpersonal relationships.

PARANOID PERSONALITY DISORDER

People with paranoid personality disorder are highly and unjustifiably suspicious and expect to be exploited or harmed by others. Based on their deep-seated suspiciousness and mistrust, they have difficulty forming close and lasting relationships with other people. In truth, they are usually reluctant to form such relationships.

Paranoid people appear cold and aloof. They pride themselves on being highly rational and objective, yet they are capable of extremely argumentative and stubborn behavior. They are also likely to be very moralistic and punitive in their philosophies and their actions. People with this disorder are prone to adopt bigoted attitudes or to embrace religious cults. They also have a tendency to be litigious, meaning that they are quick to file lawsuits against those whom they believe have wronged them.

One paranoid man sued the owner of an automobile dealership where he had recently purchased a car, claiming he had been tricked into making the purchase. Not only did he file suit, but he began to picket outside the car lot, walking back and forth, day after day, in the winter cold, even after the exasperated owner agreed to take the car back.

Everyone knows what it is like to be suspicious. Who has not experienced the unsettling feeling of walking into a room where people are whispering and then having them stop suddenly? For normally adjusted people, such suspicions are usually passed off as unfounded and are not dwelled upon. But people with paranoid personality disorder cannot abandon their suspicions. Moreover, they go out of their way to confirm them, zeroing in on any piece of evidence that might support their fears. If evidence presents itself to the contrary, as it would to a normally

People who have paranoid personality disorder are overly suspicious and mistrustful of others; they are often hypervigilant, appearing nervous and ill at ease.

adjusted person, the paranoid individual will either misinterpret it or ignore it altogether.

Because paranoid personalities are always on guard, constantly searching for clues to confirm their suspicions, they are said to be *hypervigilant*. As a result, they often appear tense and nervous. This, in turn, makes others close by equally nervous and on guard, which, of course, fuels the fires of the paranoid person's suspicious nature.

Although no one knows what causes paranoid personality disorder, parental abuse and neglect and early childhood trauma are considered possible causes. It has been theorized that people with paranoid personality disorder feel vulnerable and inferior to others. To compensate for these feelings, they use a defense mechanism called *projection*. Projection involves attributing one's unacknowledged feelings, usually negative, to someone else. Projection explains why many paranoid people aggressively speak out or attack others who do not share their views.

Such argumentative and inflexible behavior is typical of those with this disorder, as is bearing grudges for long periods of time and unjustifiably reading insults or slights into the actions of others. A paranoid person might believe, for example, that he or she is about to be fired by the boss simply because he or she was not invited to lunch with other co-workers.

Not surprisingly, people with paranoid personality disorder are reluctant to confide in others, feeling that information they impart might later be used against them. These people form intimate relationships only with those they can trust absolutely, and such relationships are usually limited to one person. Even so, absolute trust is a difficult proposition for the paranoid person. A paranoid husband, for example, might be pathologically jealous, constantly accusing his wife of having an affair because she comes home late from work sometimes.

Because they do not suffer delusions like paranoid schizophrenics, people with paranoid personality disorder are generally not overwhelmed or undone by their suspicions. For the most part, they realize they are better off keeping unusual ideas to themselves. For this reason, paranoid personality disorder seldom results in severe impairment and may go largely unrecognized.

If paranoid people are lucky enough to find a suitable working environment, they may enjoy successful and satisfying careers. Typically, these people take great interest in mathematical, mechanical, and scientific jobs involving electronics and automation. They generally are not interested in the arts or related fields.

Although no genetic link between paranoid personality disorder and schizophrenia has yet been discovered, researchers believe that this personality disorder could predispose an individual to more serious forms of paranoia or to certain psychotic disorders.

SCHIZOID PERSONALITY DISORDER

People with schizoid personality disorder have even less interest in forming attachments with others than do paranoid personalities. They show a marked indifference to social relationships.

They are extremely introverted, generally have no close friends or companions, and are commonly thought of as loners. They have developed a lifelong pattern of being solitary, and they actually embrace such isolation. Schizoids are indifferent to praise or criticism from others, and they report lacking the ability to feel strong emotions such as joy or anger. In conversation, they may fail to nod or smile to show awareness of another person.

People with this disorder have withdrawn from the world because they are afraid of the pain that could result from any kind of attachment. Often they had a childhood devoid of warmth and parents who were extremely neglectful and did not meet their most basic emotional needs. As a result, schizoids cut themselves off from others and to some degree from themselves as well. They have little interest in sexual activity, for example, and tend to deny or dissociate bodily feelings in general. "Because of a

Those with schizoid personality disorder do not have much interest in forming personal relationships. They lead a solitary life by choice and are often more comfortable in isolation than with people.

lack of social skills or desire for sexual experiences," says the DSM-III, "males with this disorder are usually incapable of dating and rarely marry. Females may passively accept courtship and marry."

In place of social interaction, the schizoid personality creates and functions within a well-developed fantasy life. "The patient seems to live in an imaginary world in which people and situations are more gratifying than in reality," states the *New Harvard Guide to Psychiatry*.

Because of their solitary nature, schizoids usually choose occupations that require working in isolation. Like paranoid people, schizoids tend to involve themselves in careers dealing with things—mechanical or scientific—rather than with people. They may work night shifts or in other positions requiring no supervision or minimal interaction with fellow workers.

Unlike the paranoid person, however, who may behave stubbornly and aggressively, the schizoid keeps to him- or herself and feels no strong emotions one way or the other. Although schizoids may fantasize about violence or aggression, they do not actually show such emotions, and they are rarely a threat to society or themselves.

Schizoid personality disorder was initially believed to be a milder form of schizophrenia. Today, it is thought that the two illnesses may be genetically related. Thus far, however, no genetic link has actually been discovered. Although schizoids share many similarities with schizophrenics, the major distinction between the two illnesses is that schizoids show reality-based thought processes and schizophrenics do not.

SCHIZOTYPAL
PERSONALITY DISORDER

The schizotypal personality disorder is new to the DSM-III. Of the three personality disorders discussed in this chapter, schizotypal disorder is most closely associated with actual schizophrenia. In fact, there appears to be a genetic connection between schizophrenia and schizotypal personality disorder. People with schizotypal personality disorder often have biologic relatives with schizophrenia. But schizotypal personality disorder is also very similar to the schizoid and paranoid disorders, and these disorders frequently overlap. Mental health professionals refer to this cluster of personality disorders as being contained within the spectrum of schizophrenia.

Schizotypal personalities isolate themselves from social interactions and close associations. These people are acutely uncomfortable in social settings, and they are suspicious and mistrustful of others.

It is not always easy to distinguish between schizoid and schizotypal people. The key difference seems to be the bizarre, almost psychotic thought processes found in schizotypal patients, whereas the thought processes of schizoids are based in reality. It is probably the presence of some sort of thought disorder in schizotypal patients that explains the closer link to schizophrenia. Schizotypal people are not psychotic, but like schizophrenics, they suffer from significant thought disorders that can include paranoia, perceptual illusions, and extensive fantasies.

Schizotypal personality disorder is the personality disorder most closely associated with schizophrenia. People with this disorder often have a distorted, almost psychotic thought process that is not based in reality.

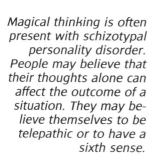

Magical thinking is often present with schizotypal personality disorder. People may believe that their thoughts alone can affect the outcome of a situation. They may believe themselves to be telepathic or to have a sixth sense.

One of the hallmarks of schizotypal personality disorder is so-called *magical thinking.* People with this disorder may believe, for example, that they are telepathic or clairvoyant. They often have the feeling of a sixth sense that might enable them to communicate with dead relatives or to predict future events. Some schizotypal patients have reported a belief that others can sense their inner feelings.

Schizotypal personalities appear more odd and eccentric than schizoids. Their eccentricity in dress and behavior is usually immediately apparent, even to strangers. Also, the schizotypal person frequently talks to him- or herself in an odd, disjointed fashion. In conversation with others, the schizotypal person may express ideas vaguely, using words and metaphors in unusual ways.

The diagnostic category of schizotypal personality disorder, along with the schizoid and paranoid disorders, has not been adequately studied. Because these disorders are so closely related to schizophrenia and because that disease is far more serious and debilitating, the personality disorders have not received as much attention as schizophrenia itself. But it is hoped that by better understanding schizophrenia, associated mental illnesses such as these personality disorders can also be better understood and people with these disorders treated with greater success.

Although a cure for schizophrenia does not seem to be imminent, the disease is treatable, thanks to a number of proven antipsychotic drugs, which are discussed further in Chapter 8. And, as research continues into the nature of neurotransmitters and the ways in which they affect behavior, there seems to be more hope than ever for schizophrenics—and those suffering from associated personality disorders—that one day a cure will be found.

•   •   •   •

CHAPTER 6

AVOIDANT AND DEPENDENT PERSONALITY DISORDERS

People with avoidant and dependent personality disorders, like those with paranoid, schizoid, and schizotypal personality disorders, have a great deal of difficulty with social interaction and personal relationships, but for different reasons. Avoidant personalities shy away from associations and social settings, not because they want to, but because they are tremendously afraid of being rejected, criticized, or humiliated. Unlike schizoids and schizotypals, who embrace isolation, people with

avoidant personality disorder yearn for the closeness and intimacy of relationships but cannot bring themselves to pursue
them. Dependent personalities are able to forge intimate relationships, but at a high cost: They maintain such relationships
only by extreme submission to and compliance with others.

Although there are no exact statistics, these two personality
disorders are believed to be common throughout all levels of
society. Many characteristics of avoidant and dependent personality disorder may appear in a wide range of normal people, from
the timid, blushing classmate who barely says a word, to the co-
worker who agrees with everyone's opinions simply to avoid confrontation or criticism. But, in people with these disorders, this
behavior is taken to the extreme.

AVOIDANT PERSONALITY DISORDER

Avoidant personality disorder is characterized by great shyness
and discomfort in social situations. People with this disorder, as
its name suggests, avoid contact with others to alleviate the anxiety brought on by social settings. Avoidants are exceedingly quiet
and unassuming; they prefer to blend in rather than stand out.
Avoidants want to be socially accepted, but because they are
easily embarrassed and are frightened about the way others view
them, they are almost never comfortable in a group.

Most people are somewhat cautious in social settings, especially unfamiliar ones. Nobody wants to say or do the wrong
thing. Avoidant people, however, are so overly cautious about
appearing nervous or embarrassing themselves that they may
not speak at all in a group situation.

It is normal enough for a person to be concerned with how
others see him or her. In fact, the opinions and feelings of role
models—those who are admired and emulated—can be positive
and stabilizing influences. But for the person with avoidant personality disorder, concerns about other people's feelings are
overemphasized and dwelled upon. The slightest criticism or
even a hint of criticism can have a devastating effect.

This *generalized timidity* also makes avoidant people reluctant
do or try things that are not part of their normal routine.
ten," the DSM-III notes, "the potential difficulties, physical
gers, or risks involved in doing something ordinary, but out-

side the person's usual activities, are exaggerated. For example, the person may cancel an important trip because of a remote possibility that heavy rain will make driving dangerous."

People with avoidant personality disorder also tend to avoid the limelight. Unlike histrionics, who thrive on attention, avoidants do not like to be noticed, nor do they accept positions of authority where they will be called on to voice their opinions. The avoidant person is so uncomfortable in social situations that he or she might pass up a promotion at work because it could mean increased social demands such as entertaining clients or speaking in public.

People with avoidant personality disorder show a lifelong pattern of social detachment. Avoidants usually have no close friends or perhaps only one, and they only attempt to form relationships when they are absolutely certain of being liked and accepted.

Avoidant personality disorder represents a new diagnostic category in the DSM-III, and so far there has been little research into the illness. Parental rejection is thought to be a strong factor in its development. It is theorized that parents who constantly criticize, demean, and humiliate their children instill in them a

A childhood filled with rejection by and criticism and humiliation from parents may instill deep feelings of worthlessness in children, possibly prompting the development of avoidant personality disorder in later years.

mistrust of others and a low sense of self-worth. With such a foundation, children may grow up feeling weak, worthless, and inferior to others.

Avoidant and antisocial people share many similarities in this regard. From harsh early childhood experiences, both learn mistrust and suspiciousness, and both lack self-esteem. But whereas the antisocial person will grow up to act out anger and aggressiveness, the avoidant person detaches and withdraws.

Why does one person become aggressive and another avoidant? One possible explanation is temperament, the predisposition toward certain kinds of behaviors. A predisposition to withdraw—possibly inherited—might promote the development of avoidant personality disorder when combined with poor parenting and other environmental stresses.

Whatever the reason, avoidant personalities grow up with a very weak self-image. They often feel empty and sad, believing they are somehow different from their peers. Like antisocial and paranoid personalities, avoidants are naturally suspicious of others and tend to expect the worst from them.

Although people with this disorder reduce anxiety by avoiding others, their anxiety is by no means eliminated. Painfully aware of their social and interpersonal shortcomings, avoidants often feel bad about themselves for not being better equipped to handle social situations or for wanting intimate relationships but not being able to achieve them. Avoidants feel powerless to seek out intimacy and to make themselves acceptable, which is what they want most.

DEPENDENT
PERSONALITY DISORDER

Like those with avoidant personality disorder, people with dependent personality disorder desperately want intimate relationships, and they make substantial sacrifices to maintain them. Extremely passive and submissive, dependents rely on others to make such common decisions as what to eat, what to wear, and with whom to be friendly. They need to be told what to do and how to manage their life, and they need constant reassurance that their actions are appropriate and acceptable.

Interpersonal relationships characterized by clinging behavior and extreme submissiveness and passivity are common to those with dependent personality disorder. Such people may have only a few friends on whom they rely almost completely.

Dependent people may limit their relationships to a few individuals on whom they can completely depend. They arrange their life so that important, and even trivial, decisions can be made for them—by parents, spouses, bosses, or friends. Dependents often choose careers and hobbies not based on their skills or desires but simply to please others.

As might be expected, such excessive dependence severely hampers a person's ability to initiate projects or to express opinions. But people with this disorder are content to submit to the will of others, even if it means losing or submerging their own individuality.

The main reason for this self-defeating behavior is that dependents do not believe that they can function without constant help from other people, so they cling to those who take care of them. Extreme lack of self-confidence and feelings of unworthiness are the reasons dependents feel helpless by themselves. Parental influences during early childhood are thought to have a tremendous impact on such feelings. Parents who reinforce the idea that independence is negative and will lead to abandonment can promote a lack of self-confidence that in later life fosters excessive dependence.

"The person with this disorder," explains Waldinger in *Fundamentals of Psychiatry*, "will put up with a great deal from others in order to preserve a dependent relationship and avoid having to function autonomously—for example, the wife who puts up with verbal and physical abuse from her husband because she feels incapable of functioning without him."

Dependents regularly take on demeaning tasks or accept unpleasant circumstances to ingratiate themselves and ensure the loyalty and acceptance of others. For example, a dependent woman might meekly accept her husband's ongoing extramarital affairs rather than complain and run the risk of losing him.

As Theodore Millon writes in *Disorders of Personality*:

A great fear of abandonment based on low self-esteem may keep women with dependent personality disorder in destructive, even violent, relationships. They will submit to much, rather than face being alone.

Dependents must be more than weak and docile if they are to secure and retain their "hold" on others. They must be admiring, loving, and willing to give their "all." Only by total submission and loyalty can they be assured of consistent care and affection. . . . Also important is that most have learned the "inferior" role well. They are able, thereby, to provide their "superior" partners with the feeling of being useful, sympathetic, stronger, and competent—precisely those behaviors that dependents seek in their mates.

Dependent personality disorder is most commonly diagnosed in women. As with histrionic disorder, many mental health professionals suspect that the diagnosis and high incidence among women is often a result of sex bias. Few would dispute that most cultures have traditionally conditioned women to be dependent on men. Until recently, the majority of women were raised with the belief that men were the stronger sex, the breadwinners, and the protectors and that a woman's job was to acquiesce and see to the needs of the man. Although this attitude is changing as more and more women enter the work force and achieve financial and career equality with their male counterparts, there is still a strong tendency—among both men and women—to believe in the old stereotypes. But even those who hold onto this old-fashioned view of the male-female relationship are seldom prepared for the excessiveness of dependent personality disorder.

The fear of abandonment is another trademark of the dependent personality. Because they lack self-confidence and do not believe they can function by themselves, dependents are terribly afraid of being alone or abandoned. Consequently, they will do practically anything to accommodate a spouse or lover to keep him or her from leaving. To the dependent's way of thinking, an awful relationship is better than no relationship at all.

This explains, in part, why so many battered wives—against the counseling of social workers, clergy, family, and friends— ultimately go back to their abusive husbands. Dependents are willing to put up with almost anything to keep from being on their own. This manifestation of dependent personality disorder can have extremely serious consequences.

An associated complication of both avoidant and dependent personality disorders is a tendency to have social phobias. Social phobias include fear of public speaking, of using public rest rooms, or of being in public places (e.g., elevators, movie theaters, supermarkets) from which escape might be difficult. Social phobias are in many ways similar to avoidant and dependent personality disorders. The person with *agoraphobia*, a fear of being in open or public places, demonstrates severe avoidance behavior by simply staying at home to avoid the anxiety and panic attacks of going out. In the process, that person also becomes dependent on others to take care of his or her needs outside the home.

•   •   •   •

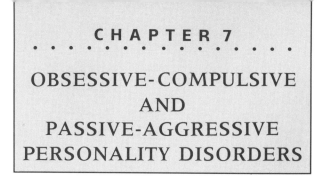

CHAPTER 7

OBSESSIVE-COMPULSIVE AND PASSIVE-AGGRESSIVE PERSONALITY DISORDERS

Woman Washing Her Hands, *Gerard Terborch (1617–81)*

Most students know what it is like to work hard on a school assignment, revising it over and over, anxiously worrying about the grade he or she will receive. Other assignments are dreaded, so bothersome or difficult that they are put off until the last possible moment.

These behaviors express two personality traits—perfectionism and procrastination—common to many students. But when such behaviors persist inflexibly, they can also be trademarks of obsessive-compulsive and passive-aggressive personality disorders. Preoccupied with minute and trivial details, the obsessive-compulsive often fails to complete tasks because standards are set too high. The passive-aggressive person, on the other hand, procrastinates and conveniently "forgets" assignments and other responsibilities because of deep-seated hostility toward those around him or her.

People with these disorders share the trait of indecision, although for different reasons. Obsessive-compulsive people cannot decide between two paths of action because they are afraid of making the wrong decision. Passive-aggressive people drag their feet, not out of fear, but to thwart and frustrate the wishes of others.

OBSESSIVE-COMPULSIVE PERSONALITY DISORDER

Obsessive-compulsive personality disorder is thought by some to be one of the personality disorders most adaptable to a career. Unlike the disruptive and irritating behavior shown by people with other personality disorders, the serious, orderly, and persevering ways of the obsessive-compulsive are often viewed as valuable characteristics in the workplace. Attention to detail and strict adherence to rules and regulations are deeply ingrained in obsessive-compulsives, making them, in many cases, dependable employees.

It is important to distinguish obsessive-compulsive personality disorder from *obsessive-compulsive disorder*, a much more serious and debilitating illness. Obsessive-compulsive disorder involves persistent unwanted thoughts and actions, such as constant hand washing and so-called checking behavior, that are often overwhelming.

In a *Newsweek* magazine article entitled "Haunted by Their Habits," severe cases of obsessive-compulsive disorder were cited in which people were devastated by their unwanted thoughts and actions. One woman in her forties

had been spending up to 13 hours a day washing her hands and her house. Before she could use the soap, she had to use some bleach on the soap to make sure the soap was clean. Before that, she had to use Ajax on the bleach bottle. And this went on and on. If she happened to bump the edge of the sink while she was doing this, this would set off another hour and a half, two hours of ritual. She didn't really think there were germs there. It was just a feeling.

Researchers at the National Institute of Mental Health have recently tested a strong antidepressant drug called *clomipramine* on obsessive-compulsive patients and have achieved remarkable results. The drug, which affects levels of the neurotransmitter serotonin at the synapses in the brain, has in many cases relieved severe obsessive-compulsive symptoms within several weeks.

It is not known, however, what benefit clomipramine might have, if any, on those people with the less severe symptoms of obsessive-compulsive personality disorder. Although some studies indicate that the personality disorder could develop into the more serious obsessive-compulsive disorder, the key difference between these two illnesses is that the personality disorder is not marked by true obsessions and compulsions such as those described above.

People with obsessive-compulsive personality disorder are preoccupied with ritual and organization. They regularly make lists and rigidly follow them, regardless of changing circumstances. These people are tremendously scrupulous. They are meticulous followers and enforcers of rules and regulations and are very sensitive to the so-called pecking order, mindful of those who are superior to them and those who are not. But because they are so meticulous and preoccupied with avoiding mistakes, obsessive-compulsives can be very indecisive. They may continue to delay important and even unimportant decisions, claiming that they must have more information. An example of such indecision is an obsessive-compulsive man who is unable to choose between several different items on the menu when dining out. Ultimately forced to make one selection, he does not enjoy his meal because he cannot help wondering if he should have ordered something different.

Such a considered approach to life makes obsessive-compulsives rather humorless and stiff in social settings. They derive little spontaneous pleasure from their life. Typically, the obsessive-compulsive's idea of pleasure is something that has to be worked for or earned. The person might plan a vacation, for example, and then constantly postpone it, claiming he or she is too busy to leave work.

Because people with this disorder are so serious and structured, they are often unable to express warmth and tenderness to others. They are frequently thought of by their peers as stuffed shirts. Their preoccupation with perfection, coupled with an unreasonable insistence that things be done their way, makes it difficult for obsessive-compulsives to sustain friendships. Because they always seek to control situations, obsessive-compulsives usually alienate the people with whom they work or socialize. Still, it is not uncommon for obsessive-compulsives to have relatively stable marriages or, as is often the case, to excel in careers.

Immanuel Kant, an 18th-century philosopher, showed many of the symptoms of obsessive-compulsive personality disorder. Born in Prussia in 1724, Kant was raised in a strict and religious household. He was serious and extremely orderly.

Author Will Durant writes of the adult Kant in *The Story of Philosophy:*

Immanuel Kant is believed to have had obsessive-compulsive personality disorder. He kept a rigid schedule, performing all of his daily activities at specific times. This sort of inflexible behavior is typical of those with obsessive-compulsive personality disorder.

> Rising, coffee-drinking, writing, lecturing, dining, walking . . . each had its set time. And when Immanuel Kant, in his gray coat, cane in hand, appeared at the door of his house and strolled towards the small avenue of linden trees . . . the neighbors knew it was exactly half-past-three by the clock.

To keep from catching a cold, Durant writes, "One of his favorite principles was to breathe only through the nose, especially when out-doors; hence, in autumn, winter and spring, he would permit no one to talk to him on his daily walks."

Not only was he preoccupied with exacting schedules, Kant was detail oriented and scrupulous about most aspects of his behavior. And, typical of the obsessive-compulsive pattern, Kant could at times show monumental indecisiveness. "He thought everything out carefully before acting; and therefore remained a bachelor all his life long. Twice he thought of offering his hand to a lady; but he reflected so long that in one case the lady married a bolder man, and in the other the lady removed from [town] before the philosopher could make up his mind."

Kant's strict and moralistic upbringing is in keeping with theories of how obsessive-compulsive personality disorder develops. It is believed that parents who exercise *overcontrol* of their children, that is, parents who excessively criticize bad behavior and aggressively demand good behavior, instill in their children a need to be perfect and highly moralistic. These children grow up learning not what to do, but what not to do.

Such children shoulder a heavy burden of guilt and can become overly self-critical in later life. As adults, obsessive-compulsives are rarely satisfied with their accomplishments. They are always second-guessing their decisions, and no matter how well they do, they always think they could have done better.

PASSIVE-AGGRESSIVE
PERSONALITY DISORDER

People with passive-aggressive personality disorder are seldom interested in perfection. Instead, they express their hostility and aggression by passively resisting social and occupational demands. The passive-aggressive employee, for example, might nod

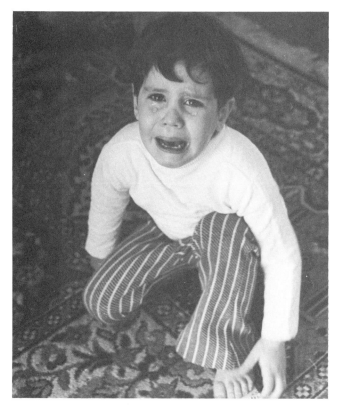

The patterns of subtle hostility and passive defiance that characterize passive-aggressive personality disorder may stem from childhood experiences. Parents who do not let their children express their independence may push the children into the behavior patterns of this personality disorder.

agreeably when the boss gives him or her a work assignment, only to put off doing the work and missing the prescribed deadline. "These people obstruct the efforts of others," says the DSM-III, "by failing to do their share of the work." Passive-aggressive personalities accomplish this in a number of ways, by procrastinating, working inefficiently, remaining inactive, or conveniently forgetting.

"The passive aggressive person's verbal expressions of compliance or agreement conceal his actual noncompliance and the secret sadistic satisfaction he derives from the frustration he thereby causes," adds the *Comprehensive Textbook of Psychiatry*. The ingrained hostility the passive-aggressive has toward others appears to be rooted in childhood. Researchers speculate that parents who exercise aggressive and authoritarian control over their children—failing to let them assert themselves as normal children do—lay the foundation for later hostility and passive defiance.

Although self-defeating, passive defiance is a clever defense. It is difficult for people to be openly aggressive toward those who hold power over them, whether these powerful people are parents, teachers, or bosses. If, for example, a child openly defies his or her parents, that child will in all likelihood be punished. So, passive resistance is substituted for active resistance. Knowing that he or she cannot be openly insubordinate on the job, the passive-aggressive employee may politely take an order from a superior and then simply ignore the order or work so slowly that the task will not be completed on time.

Interestingly, passive-aggressive personality disorder—one of the more rare and least studied of all the personality disorders—was first recognized by military psychiatrists during World War II in servicemen who passively resisted the demands of their superiors. Whether manifested in children reacting to harsh parents or army privates responding to tough drill sergeants, it seems

Passive-aggressive personality disorder was first diagnosed during World War II. Military psychiatrists identified cases in servicemen who were unable to accept the demands of their military superiors.

that passive-aggressive personality disorder is, at least in part, a by-product of people in power mistreating those subordinate to them.

Because the passive-aggressive's personality is built on a foundation of defiance and hostility, people with this disorder have difficulty sustaining or deriving pleasure from interpersonal relationships. They usually lack self-confidence and are by nature pessimistic. Often, they are irritable and resentful.

Generally without justification, passive-aggressive personalities feel that others are making unreasonable demands on them. At the same time, they believe they are doing a much better job than they are being given credit for. At the office, for example, a passive-aggressive may constantly complain to co-workers that he or she is doing all the work and that the boss is taking the credit for it.

As with most of the personality disorders, people with passive-aggressive disorder are quick to blame others for their difficulties. They are unaware that the maladaptive and self-defeating patterns ingrained in their personalities are the basis for their problems.

•   •   •   •

CHAPTER 8

. . . .

PROGNOSIS FOR PERSONALITY DISORDERS

The Madhouse (Bedlam), *William Hogarth (1697–1764)*

Throughout history, literature provides many accounts of people with mental illnesses, described variously as madmen, lunatics, or simply odd or peculiar people. In ancient times, personality disorders and other mental illnesses were attributed to supernatural spirits or were considered punishments from God for some sinful act. In early Greece, for example, it was believed that the gods could easily drive a person insane and frequently did. In the Middle Ages, the Roman Catholic church, bent on

This painting by Charles Muller shows French physician Philippe Pinel demanding that the chains be taken off the insane at Bicêtre in Paris.

punishing those who did not believe in church doctrine, claimed to be doing God's work by torturing and executing so-called heretics, who might have been nothing more than nonconformists or eccentrics. Such church-proclaimed heretics, many of whom were undoubtedly mentally ill, were labeled witches or warlocks and burned at the stake.

In 17th-century London, the asylum known as Bedlam became notorious for its ill-treatment of patients and even allowed the public in to view them as if they were part of a sideshow. Through the 18th and 19th centuries, people considered insane were imprisoned rather than treated. Asylums were prisons, and patients were often kept in inhumane conditions. One of the first attempts at reform was made at the end of the 18th century by Philippe Pinel, a French doctor. Pinel ordered that the patients at two Paris hospitals, Bicêtre and Salpêtrière, be unchained. In the mid-19th century, in the United States, Dorothea Dix, a schoolteacher, worked for better treatment of the mentally ill, succeeding in increasing public awareness. Even though most patients were no longer in chains by the start of the 20th century, they were given little real treatment, and many were institution-alized for life.

Slowly, the view that people with mental illnesses need pun-ishment rather than treatment changed. Today, knowledge of human emotions, personality, and mental illness is greater than it has ever been. And with that knowledge comes a measure of understanding and compassion for those who suffer from per-sonality disorders and other forms of mental illness.

Both mental health professionals and the general public are increasingly aware that personality disorders are diseases just like epilepsy, high blood pressure, and alcoholism. But it can still be difficult to maintain objectivity when dealing with such dis-orders. Not too long ago, many people considered alcoholics simply as individuals unwilling to control themselves. Now it is known that alcoholism is a disease and one that may even have a genetic aspect. Yet it seems easier for many people to under-stand an alcoholic's drinking or an epileptic's seizures than to understand the antisocial person who tortures dogs and cats or the dependent person who, for no apparent reason, will not go out of the house alone.

Treatment of the insane was extremely harsh during the Victorian era. "The crib," a device used to restrain unmanageable patients, is shown here in an 1882 woodcut.

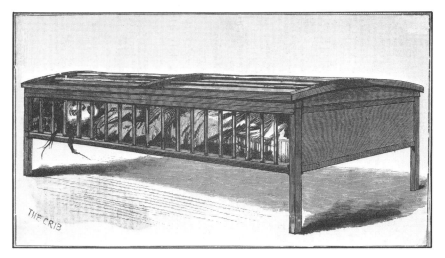

Research, especially in genetics, biology, and the brain's bio-chemistry, offers optimism for future treatments and possible cures for many mental illnesses. But although there is cause for optimism, scientists and researchers still know very little about the exact causes or progressions of the personality disorders. Most of what is believed about these disorders is based not on scientific fact but on scientific *hypotheses*, that is, on reasoned but unproven assumptions. As a group, the personality disorders have not been adequately studied, and cures for these disorders are nowhere in sight.

"Clinical lore holds that once you have a personality disorder, you have it for life," notes the author of *Fundamentals of Psychiatry*. "However, surprisingly little is known about the course of these illnesses." Treatment of personality disorders can be a frustrating and futile process of trial and error, hoping for the best, and realizing that treatment is not always successful.

Though they are less severe than psychotic disorders such as schizophrenia, personality disorders present psychiatrists, psychologists, counselors, and social workers with a unique set of challenges. Unlike other illnesses, in which patients' symptoms are generally apparent—to both patient and doctor—personality disorders can be extremely difficult to diagnose. Paranoid personalities, for example, are so suspicious that they keep their unusual ideas to themselves. And the majority of people with personality disorders are able to function in the world without ever seeking or being forced into therapy or hospitalization, even though their disorders can cause substantial impairment at home and at work.

People with personality disorders are usually unaware that anything is wrong with them. Their maladaptive and self-defeating patterns are so ingrained as to seem natural and correct. In most cases, such people are the last ones to realize—or admit—that they are the cause of their own difficulties.

For that reason, people with disordered personalities may resist treatment, claiming that they do not have a problem. One of the few positive notes about the *prognosis*, the prospect for recovery, of some of the personality disorders, most notably the antisocial and borderline varieties, is that symptoms appear to diminish with age. Still, that is only an observation with little in the way of research to substantiate it.

Demons Annoying Me, *James Ensor (1860–1949). People who suffer from paranoid personality disorder are often difficult to diagnose because they will not admit their fears to therapists.*

TREATMENT

Currently, there are two major types of treatments for personality disorders: psychotherapy and pharmacological therapy. These therapies are sometimes used in combination, and sometimes psychotherapy is used alone. Psychiatrists and therapists decide how to treat people with personality disorders after considering many variables, such as whether the patient is suicidal or violent.

Pharmacological Therapy

Pharmacological therapy is relatively new to the field of psychiatry, but it has revolutionized the treatment of illnesses such as schizophrenia and major depression. *Psychotropic drugs*, so named because they have mind-altering properties that relieve specific symptoms, are undoubtedly the brightest spot on the mental illness treatment horizon.

In 1949, a psychiatrist named John F. J. Cade found that the drug lithium could produce tameness in wild guinea pigs. Cade eventually gave the drug to several of his patients suffering from *manic*, or *bipolar, depression*, in which the patient alternates between periods of euphoria and depression. They seemed to make miraculous recoveries. One man who had been hospitalized for five years was able to leave the hospital within a month and resume his career.

A few years later, Henri Laborit, a French surgeon, hoping to find a drug that would aid anesthesia, used an antihistamine called *chlorpromazine* on some of his surgery patients. The results were so remarkable he recommended the drug (formerly known under the trade name Thorazine) to several of his psychiatrist colleagues. Administered to schizophrenics, chlorpromazine calmed hyperactive patients and, amazingly, relieved other major symptoms.

By the 1980s, fewer than 40 years after those discoveries, there was a wide variety of antipsychotic drugs available to help schizophrenics and other psychotics live and function in the community rather than be institutionalized. Antipsychotics, antidepressants (such as clomipramine), and antianxiety drugs are sometimes used for treating personality disorders, although their effects seem to be much less dramatic.

For the paranoid, schizoid, schizotypal, or borderline patient suffering from brief psychotic episodes, or for the dependent and avoidant patients suffering from phobias and panic attacks, the psychotropic drugs can be useful. Antidepressants, such as *imipramine* (trade name Tofranil), *desipramine hydrochloride* (trade name Norpramin), and *doxepin* (trade name Sinequan), and antianxiety drugs, including *chlordiazepoxide* (trade name Librium) and *diazepam* (trade name Valium), are used by therapists who treat patients with personality disorders. It is important to note, however, that the psychotropics only relieve symptoms. They do not provide a cure.

Using drugs to treat personality disorders is not always the best approach; there are drawbacks. If a patient has an infection, for example, a doctor might prescribe an antibiotic with a specific dosage for a specific number of days. This is based on extensive research and years of clinical experience. There is substantially more trial and error in prescribing psychotropics. One of the reasons is that many of the personality disorders overlap. A per-

Photomicrograph of diazepam magnified 250 times. Diazepam, known by the trade name Valium, is an antianxiety drug used by some therapists to treat certain personality disorders.

son might have more than one disorder, or the therapist might be unable to distinguish between several similar categories of mental illness. For these reasons, it is often difficult to make an accurate diagnosis on which to base drug treatment.

A further difficulty is that some drug therapies must continue for months, or even years, to be effective. This causes additional problems for the therapist whose patient is likely to resist treatment in the first place. The patient may not be able to be trusted to take prescribed drugs.

So, while they offer promise, the overall effectiveness of the psychotropics for treating personality disorders is still in doubt. In a 1986 National Institute of Mental Health study of borderline patients, for example, antianxiety, antidepressant, and anticonvulsant drugs were shown to relieve some of the patients' depression and dysphoria. But the study also indicated that "the usefulness of medications in the treatment of the disorder remains far from well established." The study calls for more research.

As knowledge of the personality disorders increases, along with scientific advances, pharmacological therapies may greatly aid in the treatment of these disorders in the same way that lithium has been used for manic depression and chlorpromazine for

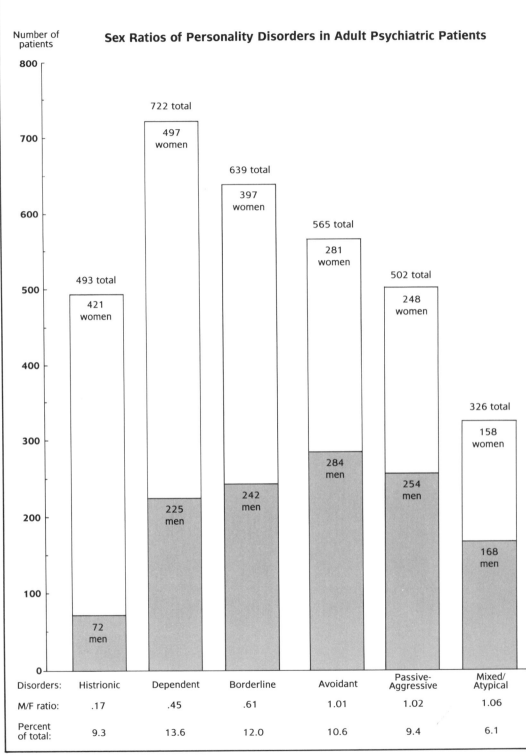

Sex Ratios of Personality Disorders in Adult Psychiatric Patients

Number of patients

800

722 total

700 — 497 women

639 total

600 — 397 women

565 total

281 women

502 total

500 — 493 total — 248 women

421 women

400

326 total

158 women

300 — 284 men

254 men

200 — 225 men / 242 men

168 men

100

72 men

0

Disorders:	Histrionic	Dependent	Borderline	Avoidant	Passive-Aggressive	Mixed/Atypical
M/F ratio:	.17	.45	.61	1.01	1.02	1.06
Percent of total:	9.3	13.6	12.0	10.6	9.4	6.1

Data from a study done by Dr. Theodore Millon.
Categories based on the DSM-III.

This study was done on a sample of 3,967 inpatients and outpatients (1,874 men and 2,093 women). The numbers and breakdown of those with one or more personality disorders (80% of original sample) are given below. In cases of two or more disorders, only the two most prominent are included. Total number of those with disorders shown below is 5,321 because, of the 3,185 people with disorders, 2,136 (54% of original sample) had two or more disorders. Of those with two or more disorders, 1,008 were male, 1,128 female (male/female ratio = .89).

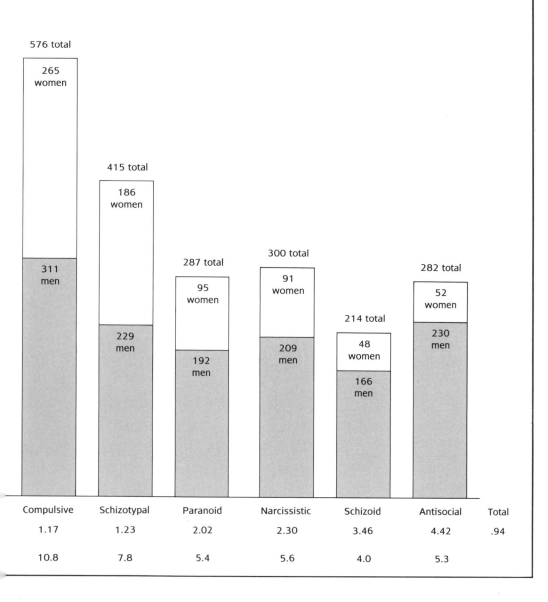

	Compulsive	Schizotypal	Paranoid	Narcissistic	Schizoid	Antisocial	Total
	1.17	1.23	2.02	2.30	3.46	4.42	.94
	10.8	7.8	5.4	5.6	4.0	5.3	

schizophrenia. But unless and until this happens, psychotherapy will continue to be the foundation of treatment.

Psychotherapy

Psychotherapy is a systematic procedure designed to change maladaptive behavior and help patients live a more positive and fulfilling life. Just as there is a variety of drugs used for pharmacological therapy, there is a variety of psychotherapies. The major categories include *psychoanalysis, group therapy*, and *behavioral therapy*, sometimes referred to as behavior modification or cognitive therapy. Different therapies are used in different situations.

Psychoanalysis Sigmund Freud developed the techniques of psychoanalysis in the late 19th and early 20th centuries. This one-on-one approach to therapy seeks to uncover the repressed

Depression or dysphoria can occur in people with certain personality disorders. These are symptoms that professionals often try to treat, although not all methods of treatment succeed.

Alcoholism is now considered a disease. Men with antisocial personality disorder have a much higher rate of alcoholism than the public in general. The male child of an alcoholic father has a higher chance of developing antisocial personality disorder than does the average person.

childhood traumas that Freud believed were the root causes of adult disorders. Psychoanalysis uses techniques such as *dream interpretation* and *free association,* in which a therapist says a word and the patient responds with the first thing that comes to mind, to help illuminate the patient's buried childhood experiences. Psychoanalysis has fallen out of favor in recent times because it can take years to complete and because it is a very expensive form of treatment. Its scientific basis and effectiveness also have been questioned. Still, the psychodynamic model of personality development upon which Freud based his theories is still widely accepted and is the basis for many current psychotherapies.

Group Therapy A more widely used type of therapy is group therapy. A therapist or counselor leads discussions among a group of patients in an informal manner, allowing interaction among members. This type of therapy is often recommended for schizoid patients because it can help them develop social skills and promotes interaction with others. Group therapy is also one of the few effective treatment methods for antisocial people, who are extremely hostile and aggressive toward authority figures. Among peers who have shared many of the same experiences, antisocial people are more relaxed. They are more likely to tolerate being confronted with their self-defeating behavior by their peers than by a therapist. Some studies suggest that obsessive-compulsives can also be helped in the short term with group therapy. It allows them to see their behavior as others see it.

There are many varieties of psychotherapy. Some are well suited to certain personality disorders and ill suited to others. For example, paranoid personalities do better in a one-on-one situation than in a group therapy setting, where they feel threatened by confrontation from others in the group. Regardless of the type of therapy, it is very hard to dramatically change the individual's underlying personality.

There are many types of psychotherapy. Some involve discussion groups of peers directed by a counselor. Most personality disorders are treated with some kind of talking therapy, alone or in conjunction with drugs.

Behavioral Therapy The maladaptive patterns ingrained during the critical early years of childhood are difficult to alter or extinguish. People with personality disorders may, however, respond favorably to behavioral therapy, an approach less concerned with the underlying cause of the disorder and more concerned with its behavioral manifestations. Schizotypal people, for example, who are extremely withdrawn and fearful, can sometimes be helped to be less fearful of social interaction through behavioral therapy in which they learn to reshape their maladaptive behaviors.

Many behavioral therapies try to desensitize patients to whatever it is that makes them anxious or fearful. In that way, while not eliminating or necessarily coming to terms with the fear, the patient can at least learn to live with it. Avoidant people, for instance, can be greatly helped by creating a hierarchy of anxiety-producing events and allowing them to confront those events one at a time in a relaxed, nonfearful environment. The therapist and avoidant patient may spend weeks simply talking about a social function such as an office party. When that ceases to produce anxiety, the patient moves on to the next event in the hierarchy. In this way, the patient's fears are slowly desensitized. This approach, called *systematic desensitization*, can also be effective with dependent personalities and those who suffer from phobias and panic attacks.

Another approach is to create what is called *therapeutic anxiety* in a patient. Because people with personality disorders often have little understanding that their behavior is the cause of their problems, they have little motivation to change. A therapist will point out the problems caused by certain behaviors, trying to create anxiety about the behavior that leads to trouble. If a patient can be made anxious about a maladaptive behavior, he or she will be motivated to change it.

Behavioral therapy is popular and widely used to treat a range of disorders. Some personality disorders, however, are thought to benefit very little from such therapy. The borderline patient, for example, can experience dysphoria for apparently no reason. In that case, it becomes difficult to find a specific behavior to modify.

Whatever the therapeutic approach, one of the main goals in treating people with personality disorders is to make them aware that their deeply ingrained and inflexible behaviors are the elemental cause of their problems. This may sound relatively simple, but maladaptive patterns that develop in the early years of life, when the foundations of personality are forming, are extremely difficult to change or extinguish in later years.

As more is learned about the personality disorders and the ways in which human emotions affect development and behavior, mental health professionals will be able to provide better answers to the riddle of personality and its disorders.

•   •   •   •

APPENDIX:
FOR MORE INFORMATION

The following is a list of organizations that can provide information about personality disorders.

American Academy of Child & Adolescent Psychiatry
3615 Wisconsin Avenue NW
Washington, DC 20016
(202) 966-7300

American Mental Health Foundation
2 East 86th Street
New York, NY 10028
(212) 737-9027

American Psychiatric Association
1400 K Street NW
Washington, DC 20005
(202) 682-6000

Canadian Mental Health Foundation
2160 Yonge Street
Toronto, Ontario M4F 2Z3
Canada
(416) 979-2221

National Alliance for the Mentally Ill
2101 Wilson Boulevard
Suite 302
Arlington, VA 22201
(703) 524-7600

National Institute for Mental Health Information Resources and Inquiries Branch
5600 Fishers Lane
Room 15C05
Rockville, MD 20857
(301) 443-4515

National Mental Health Association
1021 Prince Street
Alexandria, VA 22314
(703) 684-7722

Office of Disease Prevention and Health Promotion
National Health Information Center
P.O. Box 1133
Washington, DC 20013
(301) 565-4167
(in Washington, DC)
(800) 336-4797
(outside of Washington, DC)

Psychiatric Institute of Washington
4460 MacArthur Boulevard NW
Washington, DC 20007
(202) 965-8515

PERSONALITY DISORDERS

The following is a list of organizations and hot lines that can provide information on conditions prevalent in those with certain personality disorders.

Alcohol/Drug Abuse Referral
  Hotline
(800) ALC-OHOL
(24 hours a day)

Alcoholics Anonymous
468 Park Avenue South
New York, NY 10016
(212) 686-1100

American Association of
  Suicidology
2459 South Ash Street
Denver, CO 80222
(803) 692-0985

Canadian Association on Suicide
  Prevention
c/o Dr. Antoon A. Leenaars
3366 Dansurand Boulevard
Windsor, Ontario N9E 2E8
Canada
(519) 253-9377

Center for the Study of Anorexia
  and Bulimia
1 West 91st Street
New York, NY 10024
(212) 595-3449

Child Abuse Reporting Center
(800) 342-3720

Drug Abuse Hotline
(800) 548-3008
(24 hours a day)

Family Violence/Child Abuse
  Hotline
(800) 422-4453
(24 hours a day)

Glenbeigh Food Addictions Hot
  Line
(800) 4A-BINGE

Kemp National Center for Child
  Abuse and Neglect
1205 Oneida Street
Denver, CO 80220
(303) 321-3963

National Association of Anorexia
  Nervosa and Associated
  Disorders
Box 7
Highland Park, IL 60035
(312) 831-3438

National Committee for the
  Prevention of Child Abuse
332 South Michigan Avenue
Suite 1600
Chicago, IL 60604
(312) 663-3520

National Council on Alcoholism
  and Drug Dependence, Inc.
12 West 21st Street
7th Floor
New York, NY 10010
(212) 206-6770
(800) NCA-CALL

To receive *Mental Health for Canadians: Striking a Balance,* a mental health promotion document, write:

Publications Division
Health Services and Promotion
  Branch
Health and Welfare Canada

Jeanne Mance Building
5th Floor
Ottawa, Ontario K1A 1B4
Canada

FURTHER READING

GENERAL

American Psychiatric Association. *Diagnostic and Statistical Manual of Mental Disorders: DSM-III-R*. 3rd ed., rev. Washington, DC: American Psychiatric Press, 1987.

Cattell, Raymond B. *Crooked Personalities in Childhood and After: An Introduction to Psychotherapy*. Darby, PA: Arden Library, 1982.

Conn, Michael P., and G. F. Gebhart. *Essentials of Pharmacology*. Philadelphia: F. A. Davis Company, 1989.

Cooper, Arnold M., Allen J. Frances, and Michael H. Sacks, eds. *The Personality Disorders and Neuroses*. New York: Basic Books, 1986.

Endler, Norman S., and J. McVicker Hunt. *Personality and the Behavioral Disorders*. Rev. ed. Personality Processes Series. New York: Wiley, 1984.

Freud, Sigmund. *Dora: An Analysis of a Case of Hysteria*. New York: Macmillan, 1963.

———. *The Interpretation of Dreams*. Translated by James Strachey. New York: Avon, 1965.

Galanakis, Nita C. *Personality Disorders: Medical Subject Analysis with Research Bibliography*. Washington, DC: ABBE Publishers Association, 1985.

Gelman, David. "Haunted by Their Habits." *Newsweek*, 27 March 1989, 71–75.

Kaplan, Harold I., Alfred M. Freedman, and Benjamin Sadock. *Comprehensive Textbook of Psychiatry/III*. Baltimore: Williams & Wilkins, 1980.

Kass, F., R. L. Spitzer, and J. B. W. Williams. *An Empirical Study of the Issue of Sex Bias in the Diagnostic Criteria of DSM-III Axis II Personality Disorders*. American Psychology 38 (1983): 799–801.

Kimble, Gregory A., Norman Garmezy, and Edward Zigler. *Principles of General Psychology*. 5th ed. New York: Wiley, 1980.

Lion, John R. *Personality Disorders: Diagnosis and Management*. 2nd ed. Melbourne, FL: Krieger, 1986.

Mandler, George. *Mind and Body: Psychology of Emotion and Stress*. New York: Norton, 1984.

Meier, Michael. *A Quick Reference Guide to Using Early Recollections in Treating Personality Disorders*. Fort Thomas, KY: National Pastoral Counseling Institute, 1988.

Michaud, Stephen G., and Hugh Aynesworth. *The Only Living Witness*. New York: Signet, 1983.

Millon, Theodore. *Disorders of Personality: DSM-III: Axis II*. New York: Wiley, 1981.

———. *Modern Psychopathology: A Biosocial Approach to Maladaptive Learning and Functioning*. Philadelphia: W. B. Saunders, 1969.

Millon, Theodore, and George S. Everly, Jr. *Personality and Its Disorders: A Biosocial Learning Approach*. New York: Wiley, 1985.

Millon, Theodore, and R. Millon. *Abnormal Behavior and Personality*. Philadelphia: W. B. Saunders, 1974.

Morris, Samuel M. *Phobias and Disorders: Index of Modern Information*. Washington, DC: ABBE Publishers Association, 1988.

Nash, John. *Developmental Psychology: A Psychobiological Approach*. Englewood Cliffs, NJ: Prentice-Hall, 1970.

Newton, Jennifer. *Preventing Mental Illness*. New York: Routledge, Chapman & Hall, 1988.

Nicholi, Armand M., ed. *The New Harvard Guide to Psychiatry*. Cambridge, MA: Belknap Press, 1988.

Pascal, Gerald R. *The Practical Art of Diagnostic Interviewing*. Belmont, CA: Wadsworth, 1983.

Russell, Gerald F. M., ed. *The Neuroses and Personality Disorders*. Handbook of Psychiatry Series. New York: Cambridge University Press, 1984.

Simonov, P. V. *The Emotional Brain: Physiology, Neuroanatomy, Psychology and Emotion.* Emotions, Personality and Psychotherapy Series. New York: Plenum, 1986.

Skinner, B. F. *Beyond Freedom and Dignity.* New York: Bantam, 1984.

———. *A Matter of Consequences.* New York: NYU Press, 1985.

Snyder, Solomon H., M.D. *Madness and the Brain.* New York: McGraw-Hill, 1974.

Sue, David, et al. *Understanding Abnormal Behavior.* Boston: Houghton Mifflin, 1986.

Tyrer, P. J., and J. Alexander. "Classification of Personality Disorder." *British Journal of Psychiatry* 135 (1979): 163–67.

Tyrer, P. J., P. R. Casey, and J. Gall. "The Relationship Between Neurosis and Personality Disorder." *British Journal of Psychiatry,* 135 (1983): 404–8.

Tyrer, P. J., and H. Sievewright. "Studies of Outcome." In *Personality Disorder: Diagnosis, Management and Course,* edited by P. J. Tyrer. London: Wright, 1988.

Vinogradow, Sophia, and Irvin D. Yalom, eds. *Concise Guide to Group Psychotherapy.* Washington, DC: American Psychiatric Press, 1989.

Waldinger, Robert J. *Fundamentals of Psychiatry.* Washington, DC: American Psychiatric Press, 1986.

Watson, John B. *Behaviorism.* New York: Norton, 1970.

———. *Psychology from the Standpoint of a Behaviourist.* Classics of Psychology and Psychiatry Series. Wolfeboro, NH: Longwood Publishing Group, 1983.

PARANOID, SCHIZOID, AND SCHIZOTYPAL PERSONALITY DISORDERS

Barnes, Debrah M. "Biological Issues in Schizophrenia." *Science,* 23 January 1987.

Fried, Yehuda, and Joseph Agassi. *Paranoia: A Study in Diagnosis.* Synthese Library Series 12. Norwell, MA: Kluwer Academic, 1976.

Kohut, H. *The Analysis of Self.* New York: International Universities Press, 1971.

Meissener, William. *The Paranoid Process*. Northvale, NJ: Aronson, 1978.

―――. *Psychotherapy and the Paranoid Process*. Northvale, NJ: Aronson, 1986.

Niederland, William G. *The Schreber Case: Psychoanalytic Profile of a Paranoid Personality*. Hillsdale, NJ: Analytic Press, 1984.

Snyder, Solomon H., M.D. *Biological Aspects of Mental Disorder*. New York: Oxford University Press, 1980.

Tsuang, Ming T., M.D. *Schizophrenia: The Facts*. New York: Oxford University Press, 1982.

ANTISOCIAL, BORDERLINE, HISTRIONIC, AND NARCISSISTIC PERSONALITY DISORDERS

Cade, John F. J. "Lithium Salts in the Treatment of Psychotic Excitement." *Medical Journal of Australia* 2 (1949): 349–52.

Galski, Thomas., ed. *The Handbook of Pathological Gambling*. Springfield, IL: Thomas, 1987.

Garner, David, and Paul E. Garfinkel. *Handbook of Psychotherapy for Anorexia Nervosa and Bulimia Nervosa*. New York: Guilford, 1985.

Gibson, Diane, ed. *Occupational Therapy with Borderline Patients*. Occupational Therapy in Mental Health Series. New York: Haworth Press, 1983.

Klerman, Gerald L., ed. *Suicide and Depression Among Adolescents and Young Adults*. Washington, DC: American Psychiatric Press, 1984.

Lesieur, Henry R. *The Chase: The Compulsive Gambler*. Rochester, VT: Schenkman Books, 1984.

Lester, David. *Suicide from a Psychological Perspective*. Springfield, IL: Thomas, 1980.

Lowen, Alexander. *Narcissism: Denial of the True Self*. New York: Macmillan, 1983.

McGlashan, Thomas H. *The Borderline: Current Empirical Research*. Progress in Psychiatry Series. Washington, DC: American Psychiatric Press, 1985.

Reid, William H., ed. *The Treatment of Anti-Social Syndromes*. New York: Van Nostrand Reinhold, 1981.

Renn, Dorothy L. *Emotional Abuse of the Child*. San Diego, CA: Libra, 1988.

Slochower, Joyce A. *Excessive Eating: The Role of Emotions and Environment*. New York: Human Science Press, 1983.

Steinem, Gloria. *Marilyn*. New York: Holt, Rinehart & Winston, 1986.

Steingart, Irving. *Pathological Play in Borderline-Narcissistic Personalities*. Bridgeport, CT: Luce, 1984.

Swanson, Guy E. *Emotional Disturbances and Juvenile Delinquency*. Dissertations on Sociology Series. Edited by Harriet Zuckerman and Robert K. Merton. Salem, NH: Ayer, 1980.

U.S. Department of Health and Human Services. "Borderline Disorder: Life at the Edge." *National Institute of Mental Health Science Reporter*, February 1986.

Zionts, Paul, and Richard Simpson. *Understanding Children and Youth with Emotional and Behavioral Problems: A Handbook for Parents and Professionals*. Austin, TX: Pro Ed, 1988.

AVOIDANT, DEPENDENT, OBSESSIVE-COMPULSIVE, AND PASSIVE- AGGRESSIVE PERSONALITY DISORDERS

Beech, H. R., and M. Vaugham. *Behavioural Treatment of Obssesive States*. New York: Wiley, 1978.

Emmelkamp, Paul M. G. *Phobic and Obsessive Compulsive Disorders: Theory, Research, and Practice*. Plenum Behavior Therapy Series. New York: Plenum, 1982.

Gurian, Jay P., and Julia M. Gurian. *The Dependency Tendency: Returning to Each Other in Modern America*. Lanham, MA: University Press of America, 1983.

Humphrey, James H., ed. *Stress in Childhood*. New York: AMS Press, 1984.

Insel, Thomas, R. *New Findings in Obsessive Compulsive Disorders*. Clinical Insights Monograph. Washington, DC: American Psychiatric Press, 1984.

Nagera, Humberto. *Obsessional Neuroses: Developmental Psychopathology*. Northvale, NJ: Aronson, 1983.

Straus, Hal. "The Hemophiliacs of Emotion." *American Health*, June 1988, 61–64.

Thorkelson, Lori. *Emotional Dependency: A Threat to Close Friendships*. San Rafael, CA: Exodus International North America, 1984.

GLOSSARY

agoraphobia a disorder characterized by an intense, irrational fear of being alone, in open or public places, or in situations from which escape might be difficult or embarrassing

alcoholism a disorder characterized by a pathological use of alcohol

antidepressant a drug that prevents or relieves depression

antihistamine any of various compounds that counteract histamine, a chemical responsible for the dilation and increased permeability of blood vessels

antisocial behavior behavior that deviates from the social norm

antisocial personality disorder a mental illness characterized by chronic irresponsible and antisocial behavior; associated with personality traits such as impulsiveness, egocentricity, irritability, aggressiveness, and recklessness

anxiety an overwhelming sense of apprehension caused by tension or distress; fear without an identifiable object to be feared

autonomic nervous system the self-regulating portion of the nervous system that stimulates those muscles and glands controlling functions such as digestion, respiration, and circulation; comprises the parasympathetic and sympathetic nervous systems

avoidant personality disorder a mental illness characterized by a pervasive pattern of social discomfort, fear of negative evaluation, and timidity

behavioral dyscontrol a pathological inability to restrain one's maladaptive impulses; a trait found in people with borderline and antisocial personality disorders

behavioral therapy psychotherapy that uses any of a number of methods to encourage or discourage specific types of behavior rather than to discover the causes

borderline personality disorder a mental illness characterized by a pattern of instability that affects mood, self-image, and interpersonal relationships

chlorpromazine an antihistamine used as a tranquilizer to suppress symptoms of disturbed behavior; first of the antipsychotic drugs used to treat schizophrenia; formerly known by the brand name Thorazine

clomipramine a strong antidepressant drug that affects serotonin levels; sometimes used to treat patients with obsessions and compulsions

compulsion an irresistible impulse to act irrationally

defense mechanism any of a variety of unconscious mental processes employed to alleviate or reduce anxiety

delusion a false belief regarding the self or people or things outside the self, firmly held despite all evidence to the contrary

dependent personality disorder a mental illness characterized by extreme submission, dependent behavior, and compliance with the wishes of others

depression as a mood: feelings of sadness, despair, and discouragement; as a disorder: a group of symptoms experienced over a period of time including decreased pleasure, slowed thinking, sadness, hopelessness, guilt, and disrupted sleeping and eating patterns

devaluation an intense and extremely negative perception of an intimate friend or family member; alternating with overidealization, it is a trait common to people with borderline personality disorder

diagnostic category a grouping of disorders made on the basis of similar signs and symptoms

dissociation a defense mechanism in which a person temporarily alters or separates part of his or her identity or segregates an idea or object from its emotional significance

dream interpretation a technique in psychotherapy whereby the therapist tries to identify, in terms of psychoanalytic theory, the latent, or hidden, meaning of what the patient dreams

dysphoria a powerful combination of anxiety, depression, and anger that can rapidly intensify and cause rageful outbursts

emotion any state of strong feeling

empathy understanding for or sensitivity to the needs and desires of others

environment the surrounding conditions that influence the development and actions of an individual

euphoria an exaggerated feeling of well-being; manifest at times in people suffering from manic depression

free association a technique in psychoanalysis whereby the patient responds to certain words spoken by the therapist with the first word that comes to mind; used to help illuminate the patient's buried childhood experiences

generalized timidity an extreme feeling of shyness and overconcern with criticism that impairs the individual's normal functioning

group therapy a type of psychotherapy in which a therapist or counselor leads discussions among a group of patients while allowing interaction among group members

hallucination a sense perception unaccounted for by external stimuli

heredity the transmission of genetic traits from parent to offspring

histrionic personality disorder a mental illness characterized by excessive attention seeking, the need for approval, and exaggerated and unwarranted emotional response

hypothesis an assumption that appears to explain certain phenomena, not yet proven by experiment or observation, providing the basis for further experimentation

lithium in psychiatric medicine, the general term for lithium carbonate, a mood stabilizer used in the treatment of manic-depressive patients in the acute manic phase

magical thinking a disorder of thought in which a person believes that his or her actions, thoughts, or words may influence a specific outcome in a manner that defies normal laws of cause and effect; a symptom of schizotypal personality disorder

major depression a common mental illness characterized by a low mood extending over months, with symptoms such as unhappiness, helplessness, and hopelessness

maladaptive behavior actions that generally do not conform to accepted social standards and can cause mental and physical disorders; exhibited by all normally functioning individuals on occasion

mania a psychological state characterized by excitement, euphoria, rapid speech, flight of ideas, high energy, distractibility, irritability, and impaired judgment

manic depression bipolar depression, in which the patient alternates between mania and depression

narcissistic personality disorder a mental illness characterized by a grandiose sense of self-importance, lack of empathy for others, and a need to be thought of as special

nature versus nurture an ongoing debate discussing whether heredity or environment shapes human behavior

neurosis a mental or emotional disorder having no apparent physical cause in which the victim does not lose touch with reality; similar to a personality disorder but only affects a specific part of the personality rather than affecting all aspects of the person's life

neurotransmitter any of the chemicals that mediate the transmission of a nerve impulse across the synapse, or gap, between adjacent neurons, or nerve cells

obsessive-compulsive personality disorder a mental illness characterized by rigid, inflexible, and perfectionist behavior

overidealization an intense and extremely positive perception of an intimate friend or family member; alternating with devaluation, it is a trait common to people with borderline personality disorder

paranoia a tendency toward unfounded feelings of persecution, suspiciousness, mistrust, and combativeness

passive-aggressive personality disorder a mental illness marked by deep-seated hostility and passive resistance to authority figures and others in superior positions

personality disorders deeply ingrained maladaptive, inflexible, and usually self-defeating patterns of behavior that cause impairment in functioning and possibly distress

pharmacological therapy the treatment of mental disorders with drugs, often used in conjunction with psychotherapy

phobia a continuing and extreme irrational fear of a specific object, activity, or situation

prognosis a prediction of the course and outcome of a disease and an estimate of the chance for recovery

projection a defense mechanism in which one attributes one's own ideas or emotions to others in order to shift guilt or responsibility or to ward off anxiety

psychiatry a branch of medicine dealing with the diagnosis and treatment of mental disorders

psychology the scientific study of normal and abnormal thought processes and emotions and their effects upon behavior

psychosis a mental disturbance characterized by a loss of touch with reality or a general loss of ability to function

psychotherapy any of a number of systematic procedures designed to change maladaptive behavior and help patients live more positive and fulfilling lives; includes such therapies as psychoanalysis, group therapy, and behavioral therapy

psychotropic drugs any of a variety of mind-altering drugs, including antipsychotic, antidepressant, and antianxiety drugs, used to relieve specific symptoms of mental disorders

repression a defense mechanism in which one submerges distressing or painful ideas in the unconscious, where they continue to exert influence upon the individual

schizoid personality disorder a mental illness characterized by indifference to social relationships and interactions and an inability to feel or express emotions

schizophrenia a group of related mental disorders in which a person loses touch with reality; characterized by profound emotional withdrawal and bizarre behavior, often including delusions and hallucinations

schizotypal personality disorder a mental illness characterized by bizarre behavior and appearance, unusual ideas, and magical thinking; similar to schizophrenia but not as severe

serotonin a neurotransmitter thought to be involved in neural mechanisms important to sleep and sensory perception; low levels are thought to trigger the impulsive violence and aggression characteristic of antisocial personality disorder

sex bias an inclination within society to view certain traits as inherently male or female

social phobia a continuing and extreme irrational fear of social situations such as speaking in public, using public rest rooms, or being in public places; often prevalent in those individuals having avoidant or dependent personality disorders

systematic desensitization a type of psychotherapy in which the patient is first taught to relax and is then exposed, through his or her own imagination, to increasingly stronger anxiety-provoking stimuli until he or she is able to tolerate the most extreme stimuli

temperament a group of built-in predispositions responsible for shaping personality; thought to be genetically influenced

therapeutic anxiety a technique used to modify maladaptive behavior, such as that exhibited by people with personality disorders, in which a therapist attempts to make the patient anxious about the results of such behavior, and thus the behavior itself, in an effort to motivate the patient to change the behavior

trait an ingrained and enduring pattern of behavior that is a prominent aspect of an individual's personality

INDEX

PICTURE CREDITS

Bruce Friedland, a former reporter for the *Baltimore Sun* and editor for the *Baltimore News American*, is currently an editor for the *Baltimore Evening Sun*. He is the author of *Emotions & Thoughts* in the Chelsea House ENCYCLOPEDIA OF PSYCHOACTIVE DRUGS, Series 2.

Solomon H. Snyder, M.D., is Distinguished Service Professor of Neuroscience, Pharmacology, and Psychiatry and director of the Department of Neuroscience at the Johns Hopkins University School of Medicine. He has served as president of the Society for Neuroscience and in 1978 received the Albert Lasker Award in Medical Research for his discovery of opiate receptors in the brain. Dr. Snyder is a member of the National Academy of Sciences and a Fellow of the American Academy of Arts and Sciences. He is the author of *Drugs and the Brain*, *Uses of Marijuana*, *Madness and the Brain*, *The Troubled Mind*, and *Biological Aspects of Mental Disorder*. He is also the general editor of Chelsea House's ENCYCLOPEDIA OF PSYCHOACTIVE DRUGS.

C. Everett Koop, M.D., Sc.D., is former Surgeon General, Deputy Assistant Secretary for Health, and Director of the Office of International Health of the U.S. Public Health Service. A pediatric surgeon with an international reputation, he was previously surgeon-in-chief of Children's Hospital of Philadelphia and professor of pediatric surgery and pediatrics at the University of Pennsylvania. Dr. Koop is the author of more than 175 articles and books on the practice of medicine. He has served as surgery editor of the *Journal of Clinical Pediatrics* and editor-in-chief of the *Journal of Pediatric Surgery*, Dr. Koop has received nine honorary degrees and numerous other awards, including the Denis Brown Gold Medal of the British Association of Paediatric Surgeons, the William E. Ladd Gold Medal of the American Academy of Pediatrics, and the Copernicus Medal of the Surgical Society of Poland. He is a Chevalier of the French Legion of Honor and a member of the Royal College of Surgeons, London.